Awake to the Moment

Awake to the Moment

An Introduction to Theology

THE WORKGROUP ON CONSTRUCTIVE THEOLOGY

Laurel C. Schneider
and Stephen G. Ray Jr., editors

WESTMINSTER
JOHN KNOX PRESS
LOUISVILLE · KENTUCKY

First edition
Published by Westminster John Knox Press
Louisville, Kentucky

16 17 18 19 20 21 22 23 24 25—10 9 8 7 6 5 4 3 2 1

Unless otherwise indicated, Scripture quotations are from the New Revised Standard Version of the Bible are copyright © 1989 by the Division of Christian Education of the National Council of the Churches of Christ in the U.S.A., and are used by permission.

Book design by Sharon Adams
Cover design by Allison Taylor

Library of Congress Cataloging-in-Publication Data

Names: Schneider, Laurel C., 1961– author.
Title: Awake to the moment : an introduction to theology / Laurel C.
    Schneider and Stephen G. Ray Jr.
Description: First edition. | Louisville, KY : Westminster John Knox Press,
    2016. | Includes index. | Description based on print version record and
    CIP data provided by publisher; resource not viewed.
Identifiers: LCCN 2016022697 (print) | LCCN 2016012182 (ebook) | ISBN
    9781611646962 (ebk.) | ISBN 9780664261887 (alk. paper)
Subjects: LCSH: Theology.
Classification: LCC BR118 (print) | LCC BR118 .S355 2016 (ebook) | DDC
    230/.046—dc23
LC record available at https://lccn.loc.gov/2016022697

Most Westminster John Knox Press books are available at special quantity discounts when purchased in bulk by corporations, organizations, and special-interest groups. For more information, please e-mail SpecialSales@wjkbooks.com.

*The Workgroup on Constructive Theology
dedicates this project to every thinker about God who
transforms the world toward greater justice and mercy.*

Contents

Acknowledgments

This is a project that some said could not be done. In 2010 over seventy members of the Workgroup on Constructive Theology decided to work collectively on a project that would introduce the basic assumptions, approaches, and commitments that bring us together as constructive theologians. This project took its shape and urgency from the demand by our members teaching in colleges and universities that we speak to a new generation of students whose passions are shaping the world. Heed to this call created something quite remarkable—a moment in which seventy theologians animated by shared commitments to social justice set aside many of our differences and our own projects to do something together. Not everyone agreed on every point, of course, but every member of the Workgroup helped in some fashion to shape and support this work. It would not have been possible without each one.

During the writing of this book two long-standing members passed away. Ada María Isasi-Díaz and founding Workgroup member Edward Farley left us too soon. We were privileged to work with them, and they still help us to keep our theological focus and our justice commitments clear.

We also appreciate and acknowledge the efforts of our

editor, Robert Ratcliff of Westminster John Knox Press, for his enthusiasm for this project and his belief in it. We thank him for his faithfulness to our vision and work, and we thank the staff of Westminster John Knox Press for their dedication to quality and their patience with us.

Finally, all twenty-eight of us who together wrote this book owe debts of gratitude to our families, inherited and chosen, for their support all along every way of our theological journeys. The editors of this volume in particular appreciate our long-suffering spouses, Susan M. Ray and Emilie M. Townes, who we know rejoice with us in this moment of completion.

Introduction

The idea of God has taken many shapes in Christian history. While the diversity of images, opinions, and practices means that there have been and continue to be many versions of Christian faith and at least as many disagreements among Christians, there are nonetheless some common threads that hold together this global religion with its millions of adherents and tens of thousands of sometimes loudly different denominations. The story of the young carpenter Jesus, son of an impoverished unwed mother from the town of Nazareth in Israel, is one such thread. And the story of God, creator of *all* that is, who inexplicably became that lowly human being in a poor, colonized country, is another thread. The story of how that God reached out and still reaches out to save and empower those who suffer everywhere is yet another thread that weaves through the colorful Christian tapestry.

Theology is a kind of thinking that reflects directly on the meaning of these stories of God on behalf of the world *as it is today*. It is concerned with the many ways that Christians and others have tried to express their faith as they search for better ways to live together on this earth. It is an academic discipline in part, but more importantly, theology

1

is what everyday people do when they try to make sense of the teachings that come from their religious traditions, especially when they try to think through the practical applications of their beliefs. In the 1990s, for example, it became popular among some Christians to ask the question "what would Jesus do?" in relation to even the smallest questions of their daily lives. "WWJD" became a common acronym that some stamped on bracelets, notebook covers, or T-shirts as reminders to stop and *think* about what they had been taught, to imagine how those Christian stories and teachings might guide them in their own individual circumstances. These were reminders to those who wore the acronym on their bodies to *be* theologians themselves, to think through the ideas embedded in the sacred stories in relation to specific questions in their own lives. This impulse to make meaning is basic to theology, from the simplest rubber bracelet with "WWJD" stamped on it to the most sophisticated multivolume academic treatise, such as Thomas Aquinas's medieval *Summa Theologiae*. They are not the same, of course. The bracelet is an individual exercise, focused on immediate, individual concerns, while academic theological texts take up wider contexts and longer histories. But they both speak at heart to the work of Christian theology—the effort to understand and put into practice the meaning of Christian teachings, stories, and ideas in order to bring God better into focus for the needs of this time, this moment, this age.

Theologians take each part of the Christian faith seriously, from Jesus' strongly worded claim that any harm done to the "least" among us is done to him to church teachings on almost every subject. The point is, for theologians from the eleventh century or the twenty-first, that Christian Scriptures and ancient church teachings do not interpret themselves by themselves. Biblical scholars and theologians and individual seekers and believers interpret them. What is more, the interpretations of other centuries might not speak appropriately or even accurately to later generations—older interpretations reflect the concerns (and prejudices) of other times. This does not mean that those ancient teachings should be discarded. Not at all. They contain wisdom, but sometimes they need to be revised. Just as the question "what would Jesus do?" reflects an awareness that specific contexts require specific interpretations, theologians undertake the challenge of interpreting Christian ideas as best they can for their own age and the specific challenges that face that age, without losing the wisdom and revelatory messages embedded in the long histories and traditions of Christians who have sought to be faithful in the past.

Today our time is full of immense social struggles, new technologies, and changing landscapes. The theological challenges of interpreting Christian faith, hope, and life are as great as they ever have been, perhaps greater. We live in a world that is increasingly troubled by mass killings specifically targeting innocents; that is increasingly assaulted by racial, religious, environmental, and sexual violence; that is confronted by the militarization and enslavement of children, and more. Each of the twenty-eight theologians who came together on this project to write this book believes it is imperative that Christian theologians not turn our eyes away from this world and the challenges of this time. Christian theology, to be true to its own claims about God's intimate and enfleshed love for the world, must find its way into and through the very midst of these troubles to find the God who reached—and still reaches—to each creature who suffers and to each who dances. Theology that gets its own hands dirty with the real pain and the real joy of life in *this* very world, in *this* very time comes closer to expressing something meaningful about the God who became full and fleshly present in *that* real time and real place two thousand years ago, a place so much like our own, a place and a time as much in need of new pathways to healing as ours is now.

If we do not begin with the reality of human experience in the world as it is, theologians cannot hope to speak with any wisdom to that world. To do so, we would sound hopelessly naive or overly optimistic about our own faith in the Spirit of love and justice. It can be difficult to talk about

life having value when human, animal, and planetary life
is commodified, devalued, and destroyed in the names of
progress, tradition, purity, or profit. How do we get at real
hope for a different outcome when daily there are bombings
in marketplaces and children are slaughtered by hunger and
the abuse of neglect, when the earth itself is in distress and
whole island nations watch their ancestral homes sink under
rising oceans? How do we make sense of Christian faith in
a God who chose and continues to choose our human fate
when a simple, welcoming Bible study group in a Charleston church is gunned down on behalf of white supremacy?
Where is our basis for hope in *real* terms, not pie-in-the-sky
terms? If we take compassion for others as seriously as Jesus
apparently did, if we believe that God really does love this
world passionately, what can we celebrate and how can we
be the fun-loving people we want to be *and* devote ourselves
to steady, honest, and concrete acts of ongoing repair in a
world of so much harm and hurt?

It can be hard not to opt for easy answers or quick fixes,
to spiritualize our problems or turn them into abstractions
instead of being inconvenienced by actually changing our
ways so that others might do a little better. Jesus tells a story
about a man walking on the road one day who is assaulted
by robbers, beaten, and left for dead. Two different men
of the victim's own faith come along but cross the road
to avoid the bleeding man. Finally a foreigner, an enemy
even, comes along. He stops and helps the man, gets him
to a place where he can recover, and even leaves him some
money to help pay for his recovery![1] This is a parable Jesus
tells to someone who has just asked him what to do to attain
eternal life. His answer is indirect, but the message is clear.
What you do to help alleviate the suffering of others—even
others you don't know—is more important than who you are
or what beliefs you profess.

Christian theology that looks away from the actual harm
happening all around us is no better than the two busy
men who could not be bothered by the inconvenience of
an assault victim lying by the side of the road. If Christian

theology does not guide us to stand up for something greater than ourselves in a world of multiplying complexity, and to do so without diminishing that complexity, then it is not worth doing or studying. If Christian theology does not help us to figure out how to stand up for those being hurt who are right around us and those far away, then it is not worth doing or studying. We need theology that can help us to talk intelligently about the Spirit that moves through the earth (and the many spirits that animate us) in ways that hold together the vast and interesting differences between us on this beautiful planet.

Constructive Christian theology starts from the embodied, compassion-oriented Jesus who had the courage to live and die for the integrity of others, even others unlike himself. Constructive Christian theology recognizes that there is no point to theology, no point to talk of God, Christ, or Spirit if it does not enter fully into all of what it means to be alive and present in these days of change, wonder, and challenge.

Understanding Christian faith, the Christian triune God, is a huge theological task, one that is perhaps impossible for any one person or any one community to undertake. But trying for that understanding can be a pleasurable spiritual path, especially if there are others to talk with, to wonder with, to sing with, to protest with, to be still and listen with. We theologians seek to understand the three-way combination of the great universality of the God whom Christians and others worship, the minute specificity of that Jewish son of Mary and of God, and the rich diversity of spirit that flows from those sources in ever-widening and diversifying (and yes, sometimes divergent) communities of Christian faith. While some would argue that there should not be differences among Christians in their faith and understanding, we see these differences as essential to the evolving and growing process of wisdom in a religion that never told its stories in only one voice or only one way. Let us always remember that even the life story and teachings of Jesus come in four versions in the Bible (the four Gospels) that are not the same in every way.

What About Those Who Say That
Religion Is the Problem?

Religion is not innocent, and theology plays an important role in speaking back to our own traditions about the ways we have fallen short and the ways that we can move forward with greater attention to justice and peace, "walking more humbly with our God" as the Hebrew prophet said. This is no small challenge. In an episode of a popular television show, the main character indulged in a rant that earned the show wide acclaim on fan blogs: "Is it just me," he demanded, "or is the human race armed with religion, poisoned by prejudice, and absolutely frantic with hatred and fear, galloping pell-mell back to the Dark Ages?"[2] Despite (or perhaps because of) his role as a ruthless international fugitive going after even more ruthless criminals, the character is symptomatic of widening skepticism about the ability of governments and religions to stem or control spiraling international greed, racial and gendered violence, and ecological destruction across the planet. And in this particular scene he eloquently fingered religion for the roles religious people seem to play, over and over again, in human oppression and suffering. The show expressed a view that many people continue to hold: religion is the root cause of war, bloodshed, and suffering. But one does not have to be antireligious or hold to an atheist faith to critique religion, just as one need not be antipatriotic to critique one's government. Indeed, we contend that critique of one's own religious tradition can be as vital a part of faith as celebration of it.

The rising cycles of violence, suffering, and planetary distress are real. Something is wrong in the human world that has effects across the globe and beyond human environments. It can be a relief to pin all of that horror on something concrete and relatively simple to blame, like "religion," especially when the religions are indeed complicit in these histories. But such a simple accusation, though satisfying, may avoid the equally true complicity of religions in peace and justice making throughout history. The view that the entire history of human conflict and genocide belongs at the feet of the world's religious traditions declares that religious ideas set groups of people implacably against one another and impede scientific progress. Religion, in this view, is the source and manager of superstition blessing ignorance of the ever-changing world. Because over the centuries there have been religious people doing exactly these terrible things in the name of their God, there is good cause for such disaffection toward religions and the religious. Certainly the Christian history of Europe and of European colonial expansion around the world is liberally sprinkled with holy fervor, claims of divine right, and even, in some cases, visions of global or cosmic domination. The human history of the world is replete with Christian, Jewish, Muslim, Hindu, Buddhist, and other religious stamps of approval for bloody conquests of disputed lands, righteous invasions, violent martyrdoms, enslavement of peoples, oppressive economic systems, and wholesale destruction of cultures. In the face of this historic reality, why wouldn't reasonable people who seek peace, justice, and progress turn away from religion entirely?

On the other hand, that view ignores the fact that religious ideas have also given rise to notions of justice and to actions for peace. The story is incomplete without accounting for the ways that the religions give us the very ideas of peace with justice that enable us to stand up against atrocity, exclusion, and injustice. Movements of protest against violence and oppression go all the way back to Jesus himself and further back to the Hebrew prophets he studied, just as ideas of harmony and movements of peace exist in all of the ancient religious traditions of the world. The ideas of peace with justice exemplified by Jesus were picked up by virtuous and not-so-virtuous Christian figures across the two thousand years since. Francis of Assisi is one, the English Quakers are others, the slave songwriters in the American South and the Protestant villagers of Le Chambon-sur-Lignon yet more, and of course the Rev. Dr. Martin Luther King Jr. is another in a long list of people whose Christian understanding formed the basis of their leadership in whole movements against oppressive structures, movements that changed the world. So is it quite so simple as that: to conclude that religion is the problem, ignoring the answers it can and does give? It is impossible to separate the history of Christianity from the bad, but it is also impossible to separate it in the past and the present from the good. The very idea of the "bad" and the "good" are religiously, or theologically, implicated, as are the principles and ideas that make peace and justice conceivable.

Theology as a Practice of Truth Telling and Exploration

The authors of this book accept the reality of Christianity's complicity in the history of human suffering and believe that telling the truth about it will lead us to deeper understanding, better answers, and a more interesting faith. It is said that Jesus told his disciples one day that "the truth will make you free."[3] We do not seek to deny Christian responsibility in injustice, war, and atrocity. Just taking the examples of the Atlantic slave trade in millions of African persons that spanned four hundred years over multiple countries and the equally long assault on Native peoples and lands in the Americas—in both cases carried out largely by Christians who used religious justification for their violence—is enough to bring us to our feet in protest, anger, and deep sorrow. The fact is, constructive Christian theologians share our neighbors' disaffection with religious superiority and arrogance of any stripe, and we see religious denial of wrongdoing or triumphalist arrogance as part of the problem that we, as Christian theologians, must address even as we find within the Christian literature, traditions, and histories incredible models for courageous resistance to tyrants and resources for celebrating a world of vast diversity, beauty, and vulnerability. Our motivation for being theologians is in part our own outrage over abuses in the world done in Christ's name. We too are disaffected from those Christianities that turn away from responsibility for harm and pain in a world that needs more honesty, more welcome of difference, more compassion, more healers, and less spin. It is because of these commitments that we find simple rejection of religious ideas or of religious communities inadequate to the task of moving toward a world of peace, justice, and the open exchange of exciting new knowledge.

One of the reasons that we see protest as essential to good theology is that when people rise up—especially poor, excluded, and oppressed people—they do so because some spirit of change and hope is moving in the midst of despair. This hope and spirit of change is fragile—they can be silenced, diminished, or distorted by repressive violence. But hope and the spirit of change embodied in protest can also become a basis for new understandings and practices that actually begin to heal the world. There is always something to learn from what is happening in the world, both as warning and as avenue of hopeful and faithful religious action. This is why theology that locates itself at the center of life where the needs are greatest is also theology that actually can help to make a difference in the world.

The protest movements in Ferguson, Missouri, that erupted after the police shooting of Michael Brown in 2014 reflect a key moment in our time to which theologians who are committed to imagining God's creation must attend, since racism continues to deeply wound that creation again and again. Theologians who stand with the young protesters, not to quell their anger but to support them and help expose the historic and ongoing harm of racism as a religious concern, also help to channel the hope and spirit of change that signals the Spirit of God in the midst of their visionary demands for an end to daily violence against black persons in our society.

Another call for theological engagement in our time is the precipitous rise of religious extremism around the world, with its demands for sameness and the militarization of disciples. Religious people of a multitude of spiritual traditions, who together understand God's creation to reflect not sameness but a vast harmony of differences, must help those of their own communities to understand the challenges of living in a world of sometimes uncomfortable otherness and of sometimes unsettling changes—to understand the challenges as expressions of God's own life and existence rather than as threats to it. The terrifying destruction that violent religious extremism promotes and valorizes is a provocation to theology by theologians. It is a kind of gauntlet thrown before theologians, a theological claim that God favors some over others and justifies the extermination or intimidation of those who differ. Theologians have the choice of ceding God to these interpretations or of vigorously accepting the challenge to interpret God otherwise. It is a theological opportunity as much as a dire need.

Finally, theologians today are confronted every day with the effects of environmental distress and the global effects of corporate wealth production. The depths of working poverty into which millions of human souls are falling is not unconnected to the erosion of arable lands, loss of animal habitats and species diversity, and lack of clean water. The doctrines of profit that govern whole nations challenge theologians as never before to think through the relationship of the planet itself—creation—to the spirit of God. Christian theologians have to decide how they interpret Jesus' claim when he says he has been anointed by God to "bring good news to the poor," just as Jewish theologians must do the same with the same words by the Hebrew prophet Isaiah (Jesus was quoting the prophet).[4] Are "the poor" inevitable, or does God dwell among them, as Jesus' teaching seems to imply? Does "the poor" mean only humans, or all those creatures in God's care without voice, vote, or the means to live? Theology that begins where "the poor" live, whether in gun-ridden projects or toxic rivers (which often run past barrios and projects), must also be able to address the powers and principalities that have created those places of despair and hurt. It is not enough to say that God loves those who suffer without addressing the sources of the suffering as well.

In essence, these concerns (and others like them) lie at the root of what we mean by the term *constructive theology*. We are theologians who are not afraid to criticize the role our own religious traditions have played in creating the problems in our world today. Out of our anger and protest at Christian abuses and out of love of our Christian traditions, we are inspired to engage those traditions more energetically and constructively. We see in all of the religious traditions—and in our own traditions of Christianity specifically—many seeds of hope and wisdom for the world for which we passionately work, a world of peace and justice, a world where racism, sexism, poverty, ecological degradation, and oppression are overcome. When some of us say that Jesus, the Son of God, reveals God to us, we mean that God's intention to come close, to become human, is evident in the Jesus story. There is a divine intimacy with the world, a divine blessing of all that we experience, a faith that suffering is not the final word. The incarnation of God in Jesus Christ is an ineradicable vote of confidence in our human capacity to be better even than we think we can be, to accept God's reality in our own flesh and in the flesh of the world. It is also divine indictment of the powers that be when those powers would crush the weak on behalf of the strong. Jesus was not a powerful man from a powerful family. He was part of a despised and conquered people in a conquered corner of the earth. God showed up there, and if we say that Christian theology follows Jesus the Christ, then it only makes sense that that theology also seeks to root itself among the less powerful, to invite the powerful to that perspective, and to find divine wisdom in the conquered corners of the earth where God became (and becomes) flesh and lives among us.

This is why we do not see simple rejection of religious ideas or of religious communities to be sufficient to the task of moving toward a world of peace, justice, and the open exchange of new knowledge. Also, because we are scientifically minded, we cannot simply dismiss all the religions as error or ignorance, for in doing so we dismiss the evidence, which is the intelligence of so many millions of people throughout the world who are religious or spiritual in such a variety of ways. If we declare religious ideas and experiences entirely delusional, we disavow the lived knowledge of the majority of humankind. That is not good science or rationality. Religious ideas, or theology, undergird the meaning systems of human societies. Constructive theologians engage those meaning systems, grounded in the particular traditions of wisdom that formed us (in our case, Christian traditions). With our feet firmly planted in the present, in all that the sciences, the humanities, and the social sciences offer, we are convinced that what we have to learn from our religious traditions are pathways toward a world of healing, of justice, and of reparation for the wrongs of our past.

So constructive theology is a distinctive form of Christian theology that does not separate heavenly concerns from worldly ones. Some theologians see their work to be a careful stewardship and reiteration of sacred doctrines handed down by church authorities, and they strive to keep those doctrines as pure as possible of the messy world of politics and social struggles. But constructive theologians see religious ideas as inseparable from the fabric of human existence. We are theologians because we are convinced of the significance of religious ideas in the *whole* tapestry of human and creaturely life, and we are constructive theologians because we apply a critical lens to the many ways that Christian ideas participate in making the world, both for good and for bad. We recognize that all of theology is a blend of human and divine, of imagination and revelation. All theology is constructed out of the best efforts of human beings to understand the ineffable reality and experience of divinity in the world. And so theology always must be treated with a mixture of credulity and criticism. Like human hearts, theology is always undergoing improvement so long as it remains open.

The Bible too is always in translation (its origins are in many languages), always flowing through the linguistic and interpretive lenses of those who read it, always requiring interpretation. The fact that so many Christians differ in our interpretations does not make the Bible less the Word and words of God, but more so. God is in relation, always, to us, and we to God. And every real relationship is a living thing, requiring care, communication, and revision to correct misunderstandings. We humans often misunderstand each other; how much more often do we misunderstand God? Constructive theology starts from the recognition that we are not perfect in our understanding or our interpretations and so need always to improve, to learn from our mistakes, to build and rebuild right relations with each other and with the God who never gives up on us, no matter how slow we are to learn.

Finally, like those who would do away with religion entirely, we too are disaffected from the religions' abusive complicity in a world of hurt. Disaffection is a powerful roadblock or motivator to creative change, all depending on whether or not the experience of disaffection gets stuck in mere opposition. Mere opposition cannot see past what it opposes and ends up doing nothing beyond negation. But disaffection that leads to creative change is opposition that looks past what it opposes to other possibilities. Let's say a voter in the two-party democratic system has finally become so disgusted with the polarized negative campaigning and hollow posturing that she loses all faith in the system and she no longer wants to participate. Her disaffection could stall there, and she simply stops voting. But what does that change? Conversely, what if her disaffection leads her instead to imagine other forms of participatory democracy, and she sets herself on a long-view path toward change? She is motivated by disaffection but not stymied in opposition. She uses her disaffection to learn more, to reassess the causes and sources of the problems she sees, with an eye toward repair or toward building something better. Her no is also a long-term yes.

Like those who are disaffected from all things religious because they see so clearly a "human race armed with religion, poisoned by prejudice, and absolutely frantic with hatred and fear," constructive theology seeks to address the very religious terrors that poison us by identifying their causes and the systems that keep those terrors pumping. And like those whose spirituality undergirds and nourishes their dedication to peace and justice, we are enlivened and inspired by the long tradition of wisdom, healing, courage, and prophetic peacemaking that run through our scriptures and histories. The task, as we see it, is not to turn our backs on religious ideas, as if we could, but to engage them with all of the clarity and creativity that our disaffection and our inspiration engender in us.

The Elements of Christian Theology

Christian theologians in every age have faced large, crucial questions of meaning that face everyday people. During the period of the plagues in Europe, for example, when in some places every third person died, it was reasonable for people to ask how a supposedly good God could let innocent people die such excruciating deaths. Some theologians sought answers in lofty equations, others in revised notions of sin, and still others looked again to the story of Jesus' death as a sign of God's intimate compassion (the so-called *Pestkreuz* or plague cross is an example of this in medieval art).[5] Theologians then and now had to think through the questions that real life poses, and sometimes their answers led people to greater harmony, orientation, and sense of purpose in the face of challenging and disorienting times, and sometimes their answers failed to help at all.

How theologians develop meaningful accounts of Christian ideas has much to do with how they understand and address the signifying issues of their time. In the eleventh century Anselm famously defined theology as *faith seeking understanding*.[6] He recognized that religious articles of faith are not always self-evident. Consider, for example, the statement that Jesus is the son of God. A theologian can say that this is true, even that God has revealed it, but what does it mean? How can the theologian help people to understand it? What illustrations will clarify? What contemporary concerns will not only anchor the claim but give it life and potent meaning? Conversely, what contemporary concerns or ways of knowing will reveal misunderstandings and errors in past understandings? The long struggle of Blacks in the United States not only to eliminate slavery but also to resist and help others to resist persistent racism led theologians like James H. Cone, for example, to unmask the fallacy of Christian depictions of Jesus as a fair-haired, blue-eyed northern European. What we know about ethnicity and geography and what we are learning about racism even in our images of God matters in how we think theologically. Cone was able, through important changes in the social context of knowledge in the late twentieth century, to explain the idolatry of whiteness at work in much postslavery theology in ways that would have made little or no sense in Anselm's eleventh century.[7] But Cone's criticism grounds a new possibility for us in understanding the story of Jesus, a new understanding for grasping its imperative in a modern world still wounded and stunted by racism.

The approach to doing theology known as constructive theology starts, therefore, not only with what counts as knowledge in our time but also with how we know what we know. This is what philosophers call *epistemology*. There was a time when Europeans "knew" that darker skin was a sign of inferiority and even a mark of inhumanity. What gave them a basis for this knowing? What errors in judgment and forces in society allowed it to flourish? What kind of knowing can undo this terrible error? What unlearning has to happen? This is a theological concern for Christians precisely because whatever claims we make about God, Jesus, and the divine Spirit that moves still through the earth must strive toward that incarnate love revealed in the story of God becoming one of us. We are prone to making mistakes, particularly when money and power are at stake. And we are prone to making mistakes when the traditions of our grandparents come face-to-face with such errors and we face difficult choices of staying, leaving, or changing those traditions. And we are prone to making mistakes when we think that critical knowledge has nothing to do with faith, just as we are prone to making mistakes when we think that critical knowledge is all we need.

The next basic element of theology that is necessary to constructive theology is a deep engagement with the many traditions that hold and shape what we know of God. Theology never does its work in a vacuum and has no interest in throwing out any of the beautiful wisdom that has come down through the centuries across many different expressions of faith in community. The Christian tradition is a vast inheritance, a rich source not only of guidance and wisdom in the form of books but also of practices and communities that reveal the ongoing presence of Christ in the world. These traditions are inseparable from cultures and yet stretch beyond them as well—Catholic, Protestant, Orthodox, Pentecostal, multifaith, contemplative, and more traditions, refracted through African, Indonesian, Mexican, German, Maori, Lebanese, and more cultures, and on and on. The traditions that have shaped Christian theology are also shaped in turn by theology that speaks back to people in specific cultural contexts, in specific kinds of trouble and specific places of rich celebration. "The tradition" in Christianity is many traditions, and that is its beauty and its challenge. Theology that does not root itself deeply in what Christians understand to be their sacred traditions cannot speak meaningfully to those Christians, nor can it hope to guide them in any meaningful way toward the God for whom they long.

Ultimately, embracing both the disaffection and the resonance that characterize contemporary attitudes toward religion, constructive theology considers two primary questions: What is the relevance of Christian faith in today's world? And can Christianity help us to live well in the face of multiple threats to meaning, identity, community, and planetary survival?

The theologians who met together over the course of several years to work on this project acknowledge the despair and deep-seated worry about the future that characterize our day, and we recognize that too often, religion responds with little more than distractions, condemnations, irrelevancies, or (worse yet) beckoning the end.

In the face of such realizations, our way of doing theology stages a kind of intervention—an interruption of business as usual in order to share a vision of the world that is a different version, rooted in life and flourishing. The wager is that this version of things, this constructive Christian theology, is robustly relevant to the questions and challenges we face today. Moreover, this theology can help us live well—that is, with hope, courage, and imagination—in the midst of contemporary threats to meaning, wholeness, and material justice.

In particular, after looking at how we know and what we must unlearn in order to move toward the grace of living and loving well, and after we take up the riches of our traditions, we highlight the concrete *practices* of a life-giving, justice-seeking version of Christianity, a faith to which we gesture throughout this book. We articulate a plurality of practices for world making, for remaking the world, in the midst of significant threats to identity, community, and planetary survival. From the cultivation of bodily habits of contemplation and wonder, to rituals of protest and lament, to online community building and the daily working of the soil, the practices we consider in the final sections of this book invite you into a capacious Christianity that encourages solidarity and justice. These practices do not deny or suppress the alarming forces of greed, suffering, and violence that threaten today's world, but they stubbornly refuse to give these realities the last word. Instead, we call attention and bear witness to the resilience and palpable holiness of life.

Group writing is not easy, but it can become a practice of community building and a surprising spiritual exercise. The Workgroup on Constructive Theology responded to a call from a number of younger members that we needed to explain better why we do what we do, and how we do it, especially for readers who are perhaps drawn to understand Christian ideas but do not presuppose a background in them. We accepted this challenge to write together (rather than write separately and publish an anthology of individual essays) in order to address our growing sense that constructive theology has tools to offer to those who seek to link their spirituality with their commitments to justice, peace, and healing in the world today. The pages of this introduction lay out our passion for theology that meets the world where it lives, in all of the beauty and mess of life and in the very real struggles of each part of God's creation. Twenty-eight theologians therefore met together over the course of several years to work out agreements about the core elements of constructive theology—those agreements became the sections of this book. Each section was then cowritten by a team of theologians, tasks that required prodigious efforts at communication, listening, revising, and even rewriting as each section took shape. This is consequently a book that is truly a labor of love, cowritten by a large group of scholars whose lives and commitments cover a wide range of approaches, practices, experiences, and affiliations. The shared thread is our dedication to Christian theology that attends to the realities of this world in all of its complexity, dignity, and need for justice and healing.

Awake to the Moment is an opening and an invitation to constructive Christian theology. In it we invite you into the deepest relevance of your own life and spirituality by offering signposts for doing theology in ways that honor the struggles as well as the heart-lifting joys. We are all called to be theologians, to think through the spiritual meaning in life, to participate in prophetic vision for a healed world, and to encourage practices that move us all toward it.

What Do We Know and How?
Context and Questions

Can't take long, revelation, devastation
better stay strong.
> —Blackalicious, "Sky Is Falling"

It's the end of the world as we know it
And I feel fine.
> —R.E.M.

I s the world as we know it coming to an end? If it
is, should we be concerned, should we celebrate,
or both? In the sixth century BCE, the Greek philosopher Heraclitus pronounced that everything that exists is
in flux. "The only constant is change," he might have said.[1] It
can be exhilarating to imagine everything shifting and changing, our lives caught up in the impermanence of everything,
but no less rich in experience for all of that. But impermanence also means that we live in a steady state of endings and
uncertain beginnings.

Perhaps this is why the end of the world is such a compel-
ling idea. There are zombie runs and apocalypse parties, the
best-selling *Left Behind* series and other novels about the rap-
ture, and television shows and films that depict every imaginable planetary disaster. While it may be tempting to see this

contemporary fascination with mass destruction and the end
of things as something unique to the new millennium, it is not
new. History is punctuated with moments when people felt
everything was ending, and not in a good way. The Hebrew
Scriptures' stark imagery about the "Day of the Lord" and the
earliest Christians' certainty that Christ would return in their
lifetime to destroy the old world and begin a new one are examples from the Jewish and Christian heritage, but such ideas are
certainly not limited to either of those traditions. Widespread
interest in the ending of the Mayan calendar in 2012 as somehow signaling an impending apocalypse reminded us that many
ancient civilizations, like those of India and Mesoamerica, had
apocalyptic visions; as do Judaism, Christianity, and Islam.
And religion is not the only frame in which the end of things
might be conjured. The fields of science, history, ecology, and
economics all sometimes project vivid images of global catastrophe—whether from climate change, economic meltdown,
collapsing governments, global epidemics, terrorist attacks,
meteor strikes, or other scenarios.

In 1987, the pop band R.E.M. released a song titled "It's
the end of the world as we know it (and I feel fine)," which
made it into the top Billboard 100. We could interpret the
lyrics as bland or even cynical denial—the world is being
destroyed, but I don't care. Or we could interpret them as a
kind of optimism—the world is changing, but I'm ready for
it. Ends can be hard or they can be relief—it all depends on
the perspective one has toward what is ending, on what one
knows about the world or thinks one knows. Climate change
and environmental destruction signal ends of livable habitats,
ends that in some cases can be reversed. We know this. Really
addressing the suffering, disease, and despair that global poverty inflicts on real people (who are not statistics) signals the
end of economic structures and habits that are hard to give
up. We know this. Protests against the widespread targeting
of black men and women by the police who are supposed to
protect them signal the possibility of ends of structures of
racism, and we work toward that end. Our hope depends on
learning to see the forces that preserve racism, which is a deep

and infected wound in God's creation. Habitats disappearing signal a planetary end we fear and strive to change, protests led by young people against the abuses of Wall Street and of police signal ends we need and strive to support. In every case, "what we know" is critical to our hope and our struggle.

But notice: what we face at the end of the world as *we know it* is the point on the horizon beyond which we can't see. It is that point that drives us to ask: Where are we headed? What can we hope for? Whom can we trust? How should we act? All of these questions are essential to the challenge of being human in this world, and every human being makes choices that depend consciously or unconsciously on answers to them (even if those answers are ambivalent, or negative, like "I don't know"). These core questions of being human in the world touch on the theological category of "creation." Christian, Jewish, and Muslim theologies traditionally declare that creation is what God loves, period. Knowing what we can of the world is not only necessary for human survival and thriving, but it is a glimpse, some theologians would say, into the heart of the God whose love created and continues to create the whole cosmos and who declares it to be good.

But it is up to us to figure out just what this reality that God made, makes, and loves *is*. We bring our best scientific, philosophical, poetic, and faith-filled intuitions and skills to bear in developing knowledge of the cosmos of which we are a tiny part. Human thriving has depended upon our genius for investigation into every question that arises. What are the relations between things? What does life mean, and what is death? Why is there suffering, and what can we do to stop it? What nourishes life, and what can we do to increase it? What threatens the world and its survival? We understand the forces that undermine the survival of the human, animal, and planetary world (climate change, corporate greed, toxic waste, rampant poverty, racism, among others) and we know that these are forces that work against creation itself, and so against the heart of God. The theological idea of creation is therefore foundational to the theological question of how to approach these critical ends of the world (as we know it).

It is important to note here that "the end of the world as we know it" implies not only knowledge but also a limit to knowledge. The world is changing, that is clear. Some ends are easy to see, others are not. One way theologians understand "creation" is that God's knowing of what is and what is possible is so very expansive, the knowing in a sense spills over, generatively, into an abundant new creation, the richness of which we cannot fully anticipate. If we understand creation to begin with a fullness of divine knowledge that spills into creative surprise, we might say that our theological concern with the end of the world begins with *not knowing* what lies beyond what we have known to this point. We have to have a certain comfort level with mystery in order to remain open to what might be beyond our knowing. Understanding the world we actually inhabit therefore begins with the requirement that we recognize the limits of knowing *and* with the intuition that some kinds of knowing are better described as mystical knowing, as intuition, or even as mystery. These other ways of knowing do not serve as cover-ups but as more profound postures of openness to a "more" that the world (and God in the world) always presents. The theological challenge of understanding creation then is, first of all, the challenge of *knowing* in a way that allows for the limits of knowledge but offers hope and trust in life itself.

So, why begin our exploration of the unique character and contribution of constructive theology with a reflection on disaster movies, threats to creation, and unknowing? We already noted in the first chapter that constructive theology begins where wounds and suffering that generate protest occur, which means that theology should begin where creatures of the world (including human creatures) struggle most to live. We look to those places where young people say "enough!" to the centuries-long racism and sexism of their elders and strive to end the reign of white supremacy even as they are shot down in the streets. We look to those places where fear silences those who would say "enough!" to the extremists among them, and to the places where corporate greed grinds the bodies of poor people under its wheels. The purpose of theology is precisely to address the biggest

questions that face us as we struggle to know and to participate fully in life, at least as far as we understand them now.
Constructive theology addresses these questions because we
are committed to learn how to be present and participate,
fully, in the struggles and flourishing of all that has life.

We write in the now-ending time that is/was modernity,
which is a shorthand way of describing the Enlightenment and
the period of Western hegemony that followed. The leading
Western intellectuals of the Enlightenment viewed history as
progressing ever upward. They employed a particular kind of
scientific reasoning that they believed could solve every problem and posited an "invisible hand" that would steer even the
most selfish actions toward the common good. Since the late
twentieth century, however, the sun has slowly been setting
on this way of thinking that is sometimes referred to as the
"modern era." Who now can deny that humanity regresses
as well as progresses? While engaged in Enlightenment science and philosophy that extolled the rights of "man," Europe
and the Americas simultaneously pursued the horror of the
trans-Atlantic slave trade and chattel slavery. Meanwhile the
majority of the indigenous peoples of the Western Hemi-
sphere were decimated by colonization and genocide. Certainly the systematic murder of six million European Jews
(the Shoah) by the National Socialist political party in Ger-
many adds ample witness to the view that, left to our own
devices, human beings may always remain, as the poet Alfred
Lord Tennyson put it, "red in tooth and claw."[2] Similarly,
after we have exploded nuclear weapons and endangered
our planet we continue to ravage the very underpinnings of
the fragile ecological balance that allows us to even exist—
in order to have the newest car, the next generation of cell
phone. With this ever-growing list of examples, who could
still believe that humans are driven by reason alone? When
economies collapse like dominoes, who could maintain confidence that all people are somehow invested in the "common
good"? The earlier philosophers and theologians of Europe
who declared that human reason alone will solve all problems
were right in one thing: human reason is a powerful tool, and

it is through our capacity for reason that we can see the limits of reason, just as we see the limits of our knowledge. Reason does not win the day on its own, however. The world that is ending around us requires reimagining that runs deeper than reason. "Progress" no longer makes sense as a linear line from an indigenous, "primitive" past to an enlightened (and lightened) future when we see the racist fear at play in that scheme—"reason" begs the question: Whose reason?

It might well be that this time of endings is actually one of disorientation in which the stories we have told ourselves about progress and the myths around which we have organized our common life no longer make sense. The zombie apocalypse and Hunger Games are just stories, but they hold symbolic resonance in a time when much of the old thinking seems deadly. Zombies are the undead who devour the brains of the living. What better metaphor could we have for a time like this, when old answers and rigid theologies cause death and destruction wherever they seem to go? What sort of change in our thinking will stop the zombies?

Constructive theology is uniquely able to see in this time of endings also a time in which new meanings are built, particularly in terms of flourishing for those left at the margins in modernity. Our concern is to help envision a real future in which the forces of oppression and marginalization, what Paul describes in Ephesians 6:12 as authorities and powers, do not reassert their dominance unchallenged. All building is rebuilding; all meaning is created among the ruins of what we used to believe but now doubt, even if some new materials are brought in for the renovation. By its very inclination toward openness, constructive theology as we understand it does not expect to provide final answers. Final answers, after all, only signal ends with no new beginnings. Constructive theology isn't trying to figure out the end; it does not seek final answers, because it understands that we humans are always on the move and there are limits to our ability to know ends, even as they are occurring. Even when we think we're merely observing the world, we cannot help changing it, whether for good or for ill. Constructive theology recognizes that we are creatures of time, space, and society and that our location on these axes affects what we are able to know. So for us the task of being constructive Christian theologians is to throw ourselves fully into the midst of this radical contingency, to recognize our limitations in knowledge even as we trust the words of Jesus when John's Gospel quotes him as saying that the Spirit of truth comes to us and guides us to more truth.[3]

To those who seek to articulate absolutes that apply to all times and places, our constructive approach to theology might seem like relativism. To those uncomfortable with the idea that sacred mysteries can never be fully known, the limits of theological knowledge might feel like an intolerable constraint. But if we listen and hear the messages conveyed so loudly by events around us, we must admit that a *certain* time is ending. And in a time beyond certainty, the fact that we are entangled in the world gives us hope that does not constrain knowledge but actually enables it. We have "skin in the game" that allows us to gain knowledge about meaningful things even when absolute certainty about these things is impossible. Indeed, it is the illusion of certainty that often halts the process of embodied knowing. And it is the admittance of our uncertainty that can enable us to begin our quest for meaning ever again, engaging the world more fully in all its depth and complexity.

Mystery, then, is not a problem to solve but an ocean to sail. Uncertainty, bewilderment, doubt, skepticism, curiosity, and wonder, although they draw us to the edge of the known world, are not the end of knowing. They are the winds on which we search the universe. And we should expect to be surprised at what we find.

How We Know What We Know and Don't Know: Three Suggestions

Beginning with the end of things, and the uncertainties that endings inspire, is our way of placing our theological work squarely in the center of the big questions of life, where people actually live. We list some of those questions here and then go on to offer ideas and resources we think will help address them. These questions by no means limit the possibilities. Many others can also be raised.

- What do we do when it seems the world in which we live is changing so fast that the wisdom of our forebears means little and their traditions even less?
- What can we know about truth when everything in our culture and media seems to be no more than opinion?
- Must recognizing that there are things that cannot be known for certain lead us to do nothing because of uncertainty?
- What can we learn from *not* knowing? Does recognizing that certain things are mysteries actually help us to understand our lives and our world better?
- Of what can people of faith be certain such that we can live lives of hope and act out of compassion, regardless?

In the way of constructive theology, we consider first what resources and ways of thinking we might bring to bear in addressing these questions. In the following section, we make three suggestions: (1) that we explore giving more credence to a certain variety of skepticism in order to participate more fully in the wonder of life; (2) that we be attentive to the relationship between knowledge and power, reflecting critically on who authenticates and who mediates cultural knowledge, upon which claims of truth are based; and (3) that we recognize *broadly* those who have gone before us, who have, like us, sought to know and struggled with similar questions about knowing. What does the history of epistemology—the study of how we know what we know—have to teach us? How have our forebears come to know? To question? To doubt? To wonder? To affirm? What can we learn from them?

1. Make Room for Skepticism

A first suggestion for negotiating the epistemological concerns of our day is that we understand that doubt and skepticism can actually contribute to our knowing. As is clear from the prior section, factoring in uncertainty, when it comes to questions of knowing, is no new thing. But this might be a moment in history—particularly in the context of the shifting religious demographics in the United States—to make more of a place in our ways of learning and knowing for a kind of curious, searching, not-willing-to-believe-too-quickly skepticism that can give way to wonder. Wonder is another term, like mystery, that signals a posture of epistemological openness. Skepticism that can give way to wonder does not begin or end with a closed refusal to believe but instead operates from curiosity and a recognition of complexity, from a willingness to leave space in certainty for the "more" that creation—the product of God's love—always offers. What we are talking about in making this suggestion is not a version of skepticism that is akin to cynicism or entrenched disbelief. Rather, it is a skepticism committed to seeking and finding ways to know and to wonder.

Religious people generally have the reputation for linking *knowing* the most important things with *having faith*. And having faith is often understood as "believing without seeing." The book of Hebrews in the New Testament says "faith is . . . the conviction of things not seen" (Heb. 11:1). Jesus tells his disciple Thomas (of "doubting Thomas" fame), "blessed is the one who has not seen, and yet believes" (John 20:29). Augustine, a fifth-century church theologian from North Africa, famously instructed his readers to "believe, so that you may understand."[4] And seven centuries later Anselm, a medieval German theologian, repeated Augustine's formula in the form of a testimony saying, "I believe, that I may understand."[5]

It would seem that according to this religious tradition the appropriate order is faith then knowing, but we ask: Must one start with faith—whatever faith is—in order to know? And, if so, does starting with faith require eschewing empirical evidence, burying doubt, denying skepticism? Historically, this denial has been required for many religious people and many religious communities. The sixteenth-century reformer John Calvin, for example, generally understood doubt to be antithetical to faith. Rather than doubting in the face of suffering and other evidences that seem antithetical to God's providential care, for example, Calvin advocated trusting that God has a "hidden plan" that has yet to be made manifest.[6]

Calvin's argument no longer flies with many contemporary people of faith. Especially in modernity, we have tried to find ways of reconciling empirical evidence with our faith claims. In recent decades, there has been a resurgence of interest in and advocacy for *doubt as part of faith*, even in the context of religious communities that put a high premium on confessing, with conviction, the content of the faith.[7] There has been a resurgence of interest in doubt as a way we come to know. When we doubt, we ask questions. When we ask questions, we position ourselves to seek and to receive answers. When we doubt, we ask questions that helpfully complicate the answers we thought we had already mastered. Because doubt can help us think more deeply, richly, and complexly about what we already know, it serves to deepen our knowledge.

While doubt has gained a lot of credibility (at least among some religious people and communities) since the days of Calvin, there is currently a push to expand how we can come to know by way of *doubt* to how we can come to know by way of *skepticism*. We are using these terms more in a colloquial than in a technical sense here. What we mean by "doubt" is the experience of ambivalence in the face of what one claims to believe and what one hopes to believe again. Doubt already knows something but is questioning the content of that knowledge. Skepticism, by contrast, does not know and is unsure it even wants to. Skeptics do not want to risk believing or knowing something that turns out to be untrue or hazardous. Skeptics, therefore, tend to want to think things through for themselves before they will claim knowledge or belief. Like "doubting Thomas" in the Christian Scripture (John 20:24–29), they realize they need to "see and touch" before they can know.

Even those of us who are not skeptics through and through might learn new ways of knowing through exercising our skeptical muscles now and then. Think of Jesus' mother, Mary, in Luke 1, responding to the angel Gabriel's message that she will give birth even though she is a "virgin." "How can this be?" Mary asks, skeptically. It is this question that positions her to receive Gabriel's response, which does not really aim to prove anything to her but invites her into a new way of thinking. "For nothing will be impossible with God," says Gabriel. "Here am I, the servant of the Lord; let it be with me according to your word," Mary responds. The skepticism of Mary leads her to ask her honest question, which then positions her to know differently. She is full of wonder and ready to know and act in the world, now, in a very creative, justice-promoting way that will shortly be discussed further.

This contemporary challenge to include skepticism not as a barrier to knowing, and therefore to faith, but as a companion to knowing is being pressed primarily by those who claim they do not have faith but would like to. In US culture today, these people often identify themselves as the "Nones," or the religiously nonaffiliated.[8] Speaking of what he would like to know, self-proclaimed None Eric Weiner writes: "We Nones may not believe in God, but we hope to one day. We have a dog in this hunt."[9] "What is holding me back," he says in a PBS interview, "is my skepticism." Weiner goes on to explain that he can come "seven-eighths" of the way to faith but cannot, finally, take the "leap of faith" into whatever kind of "knowing" would ensue. The reason he cannot leap, he explains, is because he fears he might wrongly leap into something that is destructive.[10]

This is a valid fear, agree those who are aware of the ways people of faith have wielded "supposed" knowledge of God's will and ways in order to destroy. Weiner fears participating further in any way in the forces that threaten and diminish the world. He wants to be sure he is contributing to the creation, to that which is life-giving in the world. And he thinks he can do this by holding on to his skepticism as a kind of faith. To be skeptical in the face of all that threatens creation, perhaps, is to hold on to a hope that we can do better. We can know better when we admit that we can know only seven-eighths' worth, and not 100 percent.

While skepticism can be an asset to gaining life-giving

knowledge, apathy never is. Noticing such apathy decades
ago, George Lucas told Bill Moyers:

> I put the Force into the movie [*Star Wars*] in order
> to try to awaken a certain kind of spirituality in young
> people—more a belief in God than a belief in any
> particular religious system. I wanted to make it [*Star
> Wars*] so that young people would begin to ask ques-
> tions about the mystery. Not having enough interest
> in the mysteries of life to ask the question, "Is there a
> God or is there not a God?"—that is for me the worst
> thing that can happen.[11]

What is of immediate importance to Lucas is not that
the watcher of *Star Wars* comes to know God but that the
watcher comes to know that asking questions about what is
not known (i.e., the mystery) is essential to discovery, growth,
and, it seems, taking a stand against destructive uses of power.
To want to know whether God exists enough to ask questions
is to open oneself to wonder and surprise in the face of what
might be discovered. To be skeptical instead of apathetic is to
be open to knowing what can be known, even if what can be
known turns out to be something unexpected.

It might be that, for contemporary Nones, the one-eighth
"leap" into some kind of knowledge or new version of faith
could be something other than an embrace of blind trust or
unnuanced assertion. Weiner says, again, that he is "afraid"
to embrace something uncritically that might turn out to be
destructive, rather than good, whole, and life-giving. He opts,
he says, for thinking of God less as a something to *know* and
more as a "direction." This raises a question. If we give up on
knowing for fear of participating in destruction or ourselves
being destroyed, what is the loss? Put another way: What is
the cost of deciding *not to know* in order to avoid the hazards
of *knowing*?

Of course, one answer to this is that we will never know, since the only way to know would be to leap the other eighth of the way, not into some kind of intellectual knowledge, perhaps, but into a feeling, a relationship—what Kierkegaard called a leap of faith—into meeting the mystery of the living presence of an Other to see if the joy that follows is as great as some (religious leapers) say. And that leap may not result in a knowing that can ever be expressed. Mother Teresa famously admitted to never experiencing a direct relationship with God (and admitted to always feeling the lack of that experience), but she nevertheless *knew* God's love for the poorest of the poor in Calcutta. Knowing is, sometimes, not knowing or not experiencing.

But there is another answer it would benefit us to explore. As we have already noted, the global situation we find ourselves in may be interpreted as in many ways dire. It is the end of the world as we know it. How, in this context, do we know what to believe? How do we know what to do? One option is to stand back from knowing what to believe and what to do for fear of believing and doing the wrong things. Staying at a distance may feel like the only way to keep from perpetuating the forces that diminish life and erode creation in its full and thriving diversity. To cease acting because we cannot be certain might not contribute, directly, to destruction. In fact it might very well prevent us from doing the kind of harm we might do when we are overly certain but actually wrong. But to correct misplaced conviction and its associated behaviors with inaction is to shirk the work and miss the blessing of re-creating, of contributing to the making of a new world. A hazard of living only as not-knowers who by not knowing are also not workers, then, would be to allow despair to prosper.

Is there an alternative to the two extremes: knowing as embracing some form of pure, mobilizing, but potentially dangerous assertion, or remaining at arm's length from knowledge, skeptically gauging the risks? Perhaps there is. Perhaps it is to "leap" that one-eighth not into certainty, but into the possibility of all that threatens creation itself. In other words, it is not to deny, in the taking of the leap, that destruction is a possible outcome, but to hope that a creative reclaiming of the creation that has been distorted is at least as great a possibility.

One avenue for reflecting on the risks inherent in re-creation is the Christian symbol of the cross. Historically, the cross has been used far too often to fund and to justify the destruction of life. It has been used as a justification for sending victims of domestic violence back home to their abusers, reminding them they are "Christlike" in their suffering. It has been burned on the lawns of those seeking to end white supremacist laws and customs. It has been imprinted on the flags of crusaders willing to slaughter whole towns "for Christ." Shall we therefore keep the cross at arm's length, refusing to know it as our own for fear of facing our own complicity in harms that have been done under it? Or should we take that cross up and "know" it—including the risks of ending the world as we know it—in order to reshape its purposes, to re-create its meaning, and to take the ambiguities of its history into account in our own creative work aimed at restoration and healing in the world?

In Chaim Potok's novel *My Name Is Asher Lev*, Asher is a brilliant artist who is also a Hasidic Jew, which is a strongly orthodox form of Judaism. It is against the rules of his religion and against the practices of his community to draw and paint. He struggles with the members of his community—his family, teachers, and friends—and they struggle with him because he feels he cannot *not* draw and paint. They work to find ways to compromise to live together. Asher paints and draws and then violates a "line" they ask him not to cross—he begins to paint nudes because he sees that this is essential for his participation in the community of artists. Tensions mount in his community because he has crossed the line his Hasidic community has set for him, in order to be part of the community of artists. Asher's father is beside himself with the concern that Asher is participating in something demonic—instead of "mending the world," is Asher doing work that lends to its destruction? he asks. Asher's mother is torn apart emotionally by her attempts to mediate between father and son.

And then Asher paints something almost unimaginable to his community: he paints his mother on a cross. He resists doing it, when the idea first comes to him, but this destructive/creative (we could say de-creative) symbol is so powerful he finally submits to its usage. This *"goyim* symbol"—the cross that invokes the murder of millions of Jewish lives—how could Asher possibly have painted it? To his community it is even worse than painting nudes. His father stops speaking to him. He is asked to leave his community. He is asked to leave by the community's spiritual leader, the Rebbe. He has caused his people too much pain. They have learned too much about a form of suffering they don't want to admit.

Should Asher have found a way to paint the pain of his mother without the use of a cross? Should he have stood back, skeptically, keeping the cross at arm's length rather than taking such a risk? He takes a leap, in painting the cross, not into "firm and certain knowledge"[12] but into the wounds at the heart of his community, at the heart of creation. Though there is a devastating cost to himself and his community, the crucifixion he paints names the suffering of his own mother, his own family, his own community, and his own self. Though his work results in pain, it wrenches the deep knowledge of the cross out of the control of the Nazis and puts it in his own hand and into the life of the community. The power dynamic is subverted; the leap into this disorientingly creative knowing creates a new way that both Asher and the harmful emotional dynamics internal to his own community can be known and perhaps transformed. Or so Potok, the writer creating the painter who creates the frightful passage to healing seems to be suggesting. Through the image of the cross Asher paints, the community now knows not only the suffering caused when crosses are used by Gentiles to persecute Jews. They know now, also, the depth of pain they cause one another when they refuse to accept their loved ones as who they are, with all their flaws and gifts.

In his memoir, *My Bright Abyss,* the skeptical Christian believer Christian Wiman writes about how his experiences of falling in love and then finding out he has a rare blood cancer induced him to seek knowledge of God. The knowledge of God he finds changes him for the better. But it does not move him past skepticism, and it does not rise triumphant out of death and into life. Rather, it takes the possibility of creation's destruction to its heart, looking for God in the abyss itself. Wiman travels around the country testifying to why he thinks it matters to look for God in the darkness, in the abyss, in his skeptical ponderings. Some people of faith are uncomfortable with this. In one question-and-answer session following a presentation in a church, a questioner pressed him, "But . . . have you discovered a progressing state?" Wiman replied: "Do you mean have I found a resting state? A place of equanimity? No. It seems to be my fate to experience God as anxiety. My whole life is wrestling with it."[13]

Certainly faith includes doubt, and it may also allow for skepticism. After the horrors of the Jewish Holocaust were revealed (and after he lost his son to a rare blood disease and his close friend Dietrich Bonhoeffer to the death camps), and perhaps because of his unflinching determination to look honestly at injustice in the world, Union theologian Paul Lehmann was known to say that he believed in God on Mondays, Wednesdays, and Fridays, but not on Tuesdays, Thursdays, and Saturdays. He felt the necessity of both for a robust faith.[14] Skepticism can position us to respond with wonder at what can be known that we never knew about before. But it can also invite us into the possibility of losing something we value, in the course of challenging unjust systems of power, for the sake of re-creating the world. The risk of de-creation seems to us to be inherent to the work of creation. This is because certain but faulty knowledge is threatened when the Word-that-is-with-God enters the womb of a woman, or a Hasidic Jew paints his mother on a cross, or a journalist publishes truthful words those with power want to silence, or a poet dying of cancer writes about knowing God *in* the abyss.

Including doubt and skepticism as forms of knowing opens us to wondering, creating, and experiencing life and our world in ways much richer, ironically, than certainty alone would allow.

2. Attend to the Relationship Between Knowing and Power

The state of our world with its rampant poverty and seeming ubiquitous injustice begs the question of certainty about anything save cynicism. In such a reality we may ask, are Mary's words in the so-called Magnificat merely wishful thinking?[15] God lifts up the lowly, she says, pushes the powerful from their thrones, fills the hungry with good things, and sends the rich away empty. If what is being voiced here is to be taken seriously, we must rely on something other than the evidentiary approach so common to ways of knowing. To follow this approach leads necessarily to the questions, Is there ever any hope for the lowly and the hungry? Will there ever be a reckoning for the powerful and the rich?

These are fair questions, but answering them in the negative, as many self-declared realists would do, is far from innocent. The assumption that the lowly will always be subservient and the rich will always be in charge is linked to dominant forms of knowing and to dominant ways of interpreting history. We call the study of the variety of ways of knowing *epistemology*, a term that allows us to talk about knowing as a social and cultural process. *How* we know what we know involves more than memorization of facts. Knowledge and processes of knowing are culturally formed and socially maintained. Recognizing this allows us to account for differences that perspective or experience can make, for example, in knowing what one knows.

And so, according to dominant epistemological framings of history and the present, some would say, "Face facts: the powerful are the ones who will win out in the end, no matter what." Or "Might makes right." How do they know this? How does this knowing shape practices, and even history? This is not merely what some might call a "secular logic." Some Christian theological ideas are closely related to dominant epistemologies, as God is commonly envisioned not as pushing the powerful from their thrones but as sitting in the seat of power on a throne as well, at the top of the power structure. The rampant debates about the supremacy of one religion over all others in our cultural and political life bear this out.

The dominant view of history, which holds that the powerful and the wealthy are always in control, is further deconstructed when we recall that all empires have come to an end sooner or later. Religion is always part of these developments as well. Dominant religion, of which most people are aware, takes the side of the powerful and the empires. Yet there are alternative religious traditions that have taken the side of the people long before Mary's song was recorded in Luke. Hannah, the mother of the prophet Samuel, sang a similar song centuries earlier (1 Sam. 2:1–10). In US history, alternative religion supported the abolitionists, the Civil Rights movement, various labor movements, and the Occupy Wall Street movement.

We make these observations not in order to propose another dominant epistemology or regime of knowledge. Rather, we write from a position of epistemological humility. We use the term "humility" not in the generic sense that our knowledge is limited. Rather, we use it with the recognition that the world may be a very different place than the powers that be would like us to see. In other words, things are not what the dominant epistemology and its common sense want us to think. We all share in the power of knowing, if we accept that power; things are very likely otherwise than the images projected by those rulers and powers that Paul referred to in his letter to the Ephesians. Power is always part of epistemology in one way or another, but power does not have to be the power of the status quo. Our choice, like that of the character Neo in the movie *The Matrix*, is the red pill that reveals the real structures of the matrix (the structures of oppression working behind the scenes) at the expense of the fantasy.

The epistemological shift we advocate may be illustrated by talking about knowledge in relation to an object, say, a desk. At a basic level, we could discuss questions that have to do with the essence of the desk: what it is made of, its design and purpose, how much of it we can and cannot know. This is a kind of scientific epistemology, questions and answers related to scientific and philosophical methods of analysis. But there is more to know about the desk. Knowledge and power are linked in social history, and so there is the history of the desk to consider. Who made this desk, out of what materials, with what kinds of tools? These are questions that go beyond the particular company whose label is found on the desk to the labor that went into producing it and to the lives of the workers in the power differential produced by the economic system (such as capitalism) in which those workers live as well as to the natural resources used in producing the desk and the history of those resources. This is a kind of historical/political knowing: different questions yield different kinds of knowledge about the same object.

This shift to a larger epistemological frame is deceptively simple, but it has wide-ranging implications. From this broader perspective it is no longer possible to take objects at face value. We need to ask questions of how things were produced and constructed and how power flows in these processes. All that surrounds us has history, and the power that is part of everything is often visible in the form of profit that is made in the process. Not asking questions of history and power amounts to accepting the status quo as given. Simply taking for granted the existence of a desk or any other object or relationship runs the risk of surrendering to the dominant epistemology.

It is not only the desk, but our food, our methods of transportation, our homes, our churches, our books, our clothes, and so on that are produced by the labor of others, transforming natural resources and making profits for corporations. Even natural resources and nature itself are now to a very large degree shaped by the flow of power and profit. The trees from which the wooden desk was made were most likely planted by plantation workers, accumulating profit for someone else who owns the property where they are planted. Many, if not most, of the forests that exist today bear the influence of humanity. And even the forests that predate humanity were not always there; even the mountains and most other geological formations where forests grow are relatively young compared to the age of the earth. Humanity has transformed much of the planet today. The fields on which our food is grown have to be tended and worked, and the food itself is the result of thousands of years of cultivation. The carrots we eat today, for instance, are not like those found in untouched nature. The same is true for farm animals and pets; milk cows and dogs are the products of breeding that took thousands of years of work. Some of this work benefited the small communities in which it originated; some of it benefited dominant interests and the empires of past history. Large-scale agriculture contributed to the consolidation of dominant powers, as it became possible to amass wealth that could be stored up and centralized, an option that was not available to hunter-gatherer societies.

All of this knowledge has implications for how we think about religion. When we ask how things were produced and constructed and how power flows in these processes, we must not forget about religion. One of the key insights of what we are calling constructive theology is a reminder that all of our theological ideas are also constructed—none of them fell straight from heaven without passing through the sieves of human interpretations, languages, wonderment. This is not to say that theology is not inspired by revelations of God, but rather that our attempts to understand those revelations always involve interpretation. Theological ideas as constructs simply means that over time human beings put ideas together into systems of thought that they think best articulate what they have experienced (or heard, or received) of God. All theology is constructed out of the tissue of human experience of God and our genius for telling about it. Constructive theology simply acknowledges this co-creative venture, and doing so lends a particular posture to much of our work. Knowing that human beings have always had a hand in explaining and developing the meaning of experiences and words of God affects the way we read texts, our practices of reading, and our material faith. The approach of constructive theology, therefore, is to believe that texts such as the Bible, liturgical practices which constitute Christian ways of worship, and our various physical ways of being in the world are too vitally important to leave unquestioned, precisely because of the penchant of unjust power to hide in clouds of authority. As theologian Marguerite Schuster notes, "The devil hides in the structure of things."[16] So our attention to the constructed nature of theology and religion emerges from a deep commitment to the life-giving power of both and a concern about the death-dealing power of their corruption.

Religious beliefs, ideas, and practices have a history. Understanding this history, as well as the labor and the flows of power and profit connected to it, is crucial for understanding theology and religion. Religion and theology are *made*, but that does not mean they are simply *made up* in the sense of being illusory. Recognition of this fact is akin to the recognition that truth is relative, which doesn't mean there is no truth, but rather that the truths we see are related to where we are in time and space and so on. Truth is relative because reality truly is relational. Understanding the history and the constructed nature of the desk above does not make the desk less real; if anything, it makes us appreciate it more fully and gives us some options that we did not have before. When we consider desks in light of labor, power, and profit, we can choose which desks we find most appropriate and at which ones we want to work. The same is true for theologies and religions. The ones who benefit the most from the message that wealth and power are distinct signs of God's blessing (sometimes known as "Prosperity Gospel theology")[17] are the power brokers in the top positions in an economic and religious system that funnels the greatest profits upward while less and less trickles down. When we consider the flow of material resources and their relationship to messages about divine favor and furthermore begin to see theological ideas in light of the labor, power, and profit that is part of their production, we can better identify which theological interpretation and which religious tradition is more appropriate to the challenges we face at present and with which one we want to continue working. This is the beginning of truly constructive work that can lead to new creation.

The choice of which theological and religious expressions are most appropriate in any given historical moment and geographic place is not an easy one, but it has to be made in order to do constructive work that contributes to the flourishing of all of creation as best we understand it. The analytical task is, thus, linked to the constructive task. The work of John Wesley, the eighteenth-century founder of the Methodist movement, might provide an example.

In a journal entry of May 21, 1764, Wesley wrote: "Religion must not go from the greatest to the least, or the power would appear to be of men."[18] This statement, made long before the nineteenth-century critics of religion sought to expose religion as a projection of humanity, acknowledges the fundamental problem with top-down power: it shapes everything, religion included. A religion formed and sustained by top-down power reveals only human power. Epistemology does not always pick up on this problem, but when it does, the connections are not hard to see. If a dominant group of people decides to do something, backed by power and money, it is often successful. Why should we be surprised, then, when this power to shape the world applies to religion along with everything else?

The mistake of some of the nineteenth-century critics of religion was to think that these patterns of domination and subversion characterize religion in general, always and everywhere.[19] And the mistake of many of their critics was that they merely sought to rehabilitate religion, without investigating the deeper problem that some of the most common and widespread forms of religion are indeed shaped by the power brokers. They would have done well to attend to Weiner's concern, mentioned above, that we can unwittingly participate in destruction in the name of faith.

There is an alternative to top-down, power-dominant religion. As a religious reformer Wesley was not only aware of it; he was involved in it. After having warned that religion must not flow from the powerful to the powerless, he noted that there is also a religion that moves from the bottom up: "'They shall all know me,' saith the Lord, not from the greatest to the least (this is that wisdom of the world which is foolishness with God) but 'from the least to the greatest,' that the praise may not be of men, but of God."[20] When knowledge of God starts among the powerless and only then works its way to the powerful, Wesley said, that's a sure sign that it comes from God. This way of knowing God from the bottom up is what can be called "grace under pressure."[21]

What Wesley put into words over two centuries ago, linked to his reading of the Bible and to his observation of and participation in alternative religious expressions, is often forgotten today when religion is discussed. Popular confrontations between atheists (those who believe no gods or God exist) and theists (those who do) focus on dominant religion shaped by dominant powers, including dominant religious ideas of God's existence, divine omnipotence, intelligent design, and transcendence. What so many critics and supporters of religion overlook in their arguments is that it is possible to define divine power differently, not as absolute control at work from the top down or aloof from the intimate realities of this world. Indeed, we Christian theologians argue along with Wesley that these coercive kinds of powers are not divine at all. In Christianity, another definition of divine power finds expression in Jesus Christ, a laborer whose trade was carpentry and whose life and ministry was not spent among the powerful. In other religions, there are alternative traditions that push in these directions as well, like divine wisdom in Judaism and an emphasis on God's justice on the side of working people in Islam.

As a result, an appreciation for religion does not have to go hand in hand with accepting the logic of dominant ways of knowing. In fact, an awareness of religion in its alternative expressions opens the door to an alternative epistemology, which invites people to open their eyes to history and power rather than keeping them closed. When we attend to how knowledge is brokered and mediated in our society, we begin to look for bodies of knowledge that have been suppressed. We begin to ask: What are we encouraged to know and what are we encouraged to overlook? By whom? And most importantly to us, how is knowledge that subverts oppressive power struggles discovered, learned, and shared?

3. Learn from Others in History Who Have Thought about Knowing

"Is anybody hungry?" This is the first question Professor Craigo-Snell asks her students in a course she teaches. At 10:00 a.m. in a room full of undergraduates, several affirmative answers are given. The next question is, "How do you know you are hungry?" The responses are varied but predictable: "I'm light-headed," "My stomach feels funny," "I can't think straight," and sometimes a gesture toward the belly— "I feel it here." A second question is asked: "Is anybody in love?" A few brave souls say yes. "How do you know you are in love?" While the answers to this question are less predictable, over several years of teaching there has been reliable overlap between evidence of hunger and signs of love. Both involve sensations in the stomach, difficulty concentrating, and a light-headed effect. Yet students laugh when it is suggested they are mistaking hunger for love or love for hunger.

This exercise introduces the very tricky question, how do we know what we know? And how do we know what can't be known? These questions have been central preoccupations of Christian thought in Europe and North America for the past four hundred years. People of faith are not alone in asking them. Questions about how we know (epistemology) have been dominant in many fields of study.

One way of narrating how epistemology became such a concern in theological inquiry is to look back at René Descartes, using him as a stand-in demarcation for a complex shift in thought. Descartes was a French philosopher who lived from 1596 to 1650. This was an exciting and frightening time in Europe. Extended warfare, in which religion played key roles, made the social, political, and church authorities that had guided life before then seem inadequate. The old ways of doing things were not working well, and prior perspectives seemed unable to address the current problems. At the same time, the scientific revolution was getting started. Galileo looked through his telescope and saw that Earth revolves around the sun, challenging commonly held views about the place of humanity in the universe, the structure of the solar system, and the best methods for scientific inquiry. The old intellectual authorities were mistaken. On the one hand, it was scary and disconcerting to see the prior systems start to crumble. On the other hand, it was exciting to imagine all that could be learned and accomplished. In the midst of this tumultuous era, Descartes believed certainty was possible. He wanted knowledge built on a firm foundation that would not crumble under new insights.[22]

Descartes wanted to know everything with the same kind of certainty that he knew that the interior angles of a triangle always add up to 180 degrees. Such knowledge is possible, he thought, but it often gets muddled by other things in our lives. So Descartes attempted to distract himself from things that might interfere with his thinking, including his own embodied reality, his community, his ethical commitments, and his emotions. To achieve certainty, Descartes developed a method of inquiry that relied heavily on doubt. He wanted to doubt everything that he had been taught, to doubt his own cultural assumptions, and to doubt his senses. Whatever could remain after thorough doubting would be a firm foundation for knowledge.[23] What Descartes arrived at for his indubitable starting point was his own thinking: "I think, therefore I am."[24]

Yet there were a few assumptions so deeply embedded in Descartes that he did not think to doubt them. One of these is that diversity of opinion implies error: the idea that, if two people disagree about something, one of them is wrong.[25] For Descartes, Truth is objective and universal, never controvertible, written with a capital *T*. The result of a scientific experiment should be the same in Connecticut or Calcutta, Minnesota or Malta. That is the kind of certainty Descartes, and much of modern thought, values. Another assumption is that it is possible to abstract oneself from our cultural and social locations and to see with unbiased eyes.

Descartes thought he could peel back the layers of external influence to get to the solid core of his own reason, untainted by culture. A third assumption Descartes did not fully question is that the human mind is distinct, separable, and in some ways independent of the human body.[26]

In recent decades all of these assumptions have been questioned by academics in both the humanities and the sciences. Postmodernism, for instance, celebrates the possibility that truth is not singular or static, emphasizes that how we see the world is greatly influenced by our own social location, and suggests that perhaps there is not a pure core of human rationality untouched by culture. In 1983, psychologist Howard Gardner published *Frames of Mind: The Theory of Multiple Intelligences*, in which he argues that there are multiple forms of learning and processing knowledge, including bodily, visual, interpersonal, and musical. [27] How we know, Gardner suggests, cannot be reduced to a singular rationality that is distanced from emotion, embodiment, ethics, and community. His work paved the way for the term "emotional intelligence" to enter our common lexicon. Antonio Damasio, a professor of psychology, neuroscience, and neurology, published an influential text in 1994 called *Descartes' Error: Emotion, Reason and the Brain*. He explores how emotions and biology are involved in human decision making.[28] There is growing multidisciplinary research in embodied cognition, that is, how human embodiment and cognition are intertwined.[29] Our bodily gestures, facial expressions, and interactions with others change how and what we know. Our environment—from lighting to music to time pressures—affects our knowing. Power relations and cultural biases are other aspects of our environment that influence how and what we know.

We live in a moment of transition regarding what and how we know anything. These criticisms of Descartes have been so pervasive that few contemporary students would pronounce themselves Cartesian or accept his stated conclusions. At the same time, Descartes's influence is so deeply inscribed in college courses that we often do not even notice it. For example, on the first day of the class described above—before they start talking about hunger and love—students file in and sit in rows of desks that are bolted to the floor. The desks prevent group movement and foster the pretense that their bodies are not needed for this work. Having successfully carried their brains into the room, their bodies should now be forgotten. Whatever else is going on in their lives that morning, in a traditional modern classroom, students are expected to set all that aside so they can focus their rational minds on the subject at hand. Although there are many people in the room, each desk faces forward, discouraging conversation among students. Through everything from classroom etiquette to architecture, students are taught to do as Descartes did— to abstract themselves from emotions, embodiment, ethical commitments, and community—in order to learn.

In this transitional time, some researchers are focusing on how we know in less individual settings. For example, performance theorist Diana Taylor looks at how societies learn, store, and transfer knowledge. She distinguishes between two ways in which this is done. One way knowledge is learned, stored, and transferred is through the archive. "Archive" here refers to written inscriptions. By way of the archive, texts are passed on to others and read. Another way knowledge is acquired and dispersed is through the repertoire. "Repertoire" refers to physical behaviors that are regularly enacted. By way of the repertoire, knowledge can be learned, stored, and transferred through embodied, communal performances.[30] Think of learning how to do a particular dance or how to play basketball. Think of learning to feed your children in a war zone, or learning how to have self-worth in a society that despises the color of your skin or the clothes you can afford.

The work of sociologist Paul Connerton adds to this analysis. Connerton looks at how societies pass along social memories from one generation to the next. He identifies commemorative events as moments of transfer in which social memories are formed through ritual performances.[31] When we engage in communal bodily practices—such as going to a Fourth of July parade and waving American flags as veterans march by—we in some sense ratify our belief in particular understandings of reality that are stored and transferred in the practices.[32]

The lines between archive and repertoire are often blurred, as many social performances include texts. Yet the conceptual distinction allows Taylor to acknowledge and value ways of knowing that have been ignored or obscured in the modern period, during which the archive has reigned supreme. Since Descartes, students reading textbooks have been more often associated with knowledge than have athletes on a basketball court, dancers on a stage, survivors of war or oppression.[33] Children and teenagers in the United States are routinely tested on their archival knowledge, while athletes and dancers are praised for skill, talent, and agility, and survivors not at all.

Furthermore, Taylor analyzes how the determination of what counts as knowledge is related to power. Often, those who hold power have a strong influence on what is considered knowledge. Any given epistemology has both beneficiaries and casualties. In particular, Taylor looks at epistemology in light of the history of colonialism. Europeans arrived in foreign lands and announced that the natives were ignorant, uneducated people. They refused to recognize the knowledge they encountered. One of the ways they did this was to see their own archive as the only form of knowledge (and to quickly dismiss languages they did not understand). Separating their archive from repertoire, then elevating it over repertoire, served the interests of the colonizers because "written culture then, as now, seemed easier to control than embodied culture."[34] Texts could be censored, and the capacity to write could be limited to an educated elite.[35] In such contexts, declaring archives to be the only or primary space of knowledge effectively limited access to the power of knowledge (expertise, insight, argumentation, and so forth) to the lettered few.

Performance theorist Dwight Conquergood names the separation of archive and repertoire as a harmful power play, and the elevation of the archive as the location of knowledge as an ongoing buttress to hierarchies of class, race, and gender. He writes, "the hegemony of textualism" upholds "the supremacy of Western knowledge systems by erasing the vast realm of human knowledge and meaningful action that is unlettered."[36] Conquergood does not want simply to flip the hierarchy by elevating repertoire but rather to reject the separation of different forms of knowledge.[37] Cartesian epistemology, with its dualism between mind and body, contributes to a context in which it might seem logical to grant privilege to certain types of knowledge. It has similar beneficiaries and casualties. If the best form of knowledge is truth with a capital *T*, and this knowledge is learned abstraction from embodiment, then the best knowers are people whose embodiment can most readily be ignored. In the modern West, that has largely been white men with enough money and power to overlook matters of the body for the sake of wielding power over those whose bodies most often put them at a disadvantage—women and men of color and white women. For a long list of reasons rooted in sexism, racism, and heterosexism, people in socially subordinate positions are more associated with the body than the mind—including women, Blacks, and manual laborers—and so historically have seemed like poorer knowers. Given the importance of human rationality in Descartes's understanding of what it is to be human, such non-knowers have often been identified as slightly less human.

How have the changing winds of epistemology in the past four hundred years played out in Christianity? There are many ways in which more recent theories of knowledge, particularly those put forward by performance theorists such as Taylor and Conquergood, seem to fit with Christianity better than the earlier, Cartesian model. Christianity is, after all, about bodies, even if this is often overlooked. The biblical stories center on bodies—hungry, thirsty, and broken, pregnant, tortured, and raised from the dead. Furthermore, Christians learn and interpret these stories through embodied, communal activities. These include ritual actions, such as washing feet, breaking bread, and singing, as well as ethical practices, such as feeding the hungry, visiting the sick, and comforting the afflicted. In many ways, Christianity seems to be all about the stuff Descartes wanted to avoid in order to know with certainty!

It would make sense, then, to imagine that Christian thinkers rejected Descartes's epistemology, since it could not account for the fullness of knowledge that takes place in Christian life and worship. However, many Christians (particularly Protestants) try to explain how Christianity fits within the kind of knowledge that Descartes valued. They do not focus on bodies and rituals at the heart of Christianity. One example of this is John Locke, who described Christianity as profoundly reasonable. He did this, in part, by defining Christian faith as intellectual assent to propositional truth claims.[38] In Locke's writings, Christianity is much more about the rational mind than it is about embodied, communal practices. Locke was not alone in his efforts to make Christianity fit the dominant epistemology. Many others tried to reduce Christianity to essential beliefs that could be rationally affirmed. This meant saying that the embodied, communal, and ritualistic parts of Christianity were not central to faith.

Recognizing the limits of a Cartesian frame of understanding, other thinkers argue that Christianity operates in a different sphere of knowledge than the physical and social sciences. This could be the realm of ethics or feeling. But these approaches do not escape the Cartesian difficulties altogether. This is because they treat the kind of knowing granted to religion as less certain or more limited than the very best kind of knowledge, the Truth that Descartes desired. Furthermore, even in these epistemologies what takes place in Christian rituals and life is hard to describe as knowledge at all. This is unfortunate, given our recognition that what happens in liturgy is often a guiding norm for Christian thought and religious understanding. *Lex orandi, lex credendi* is a very old principle of Christianity. It means that the law of praying and worshiping (*lex orandi*) is (that is, shapes and informs) the law of believing, or theology (*lex credendi*).

Emerging in the latter half of the twentieth century, liberation theologies brought a different spin to epistemology by attending carefully to issues of power. Engaging with traditions informed by the Black Church tradition, Roman Catholic social teachings, and popular engagements with Marxian theory, liberation theologians critique claims to disembodied knowledge. As noted previously, disembodied knowing privileges those whose bodies are not already seen to be stumbling blocks to intellectual ability. This is not only unjust—it severely limits our understanding of God, of ourselves, and of our societies. Liberation theologians argue that our actions in the world profoundly shape how we know God. They are not speaking directly to liturgical actions but rather to actions of solidarity with the oppressed and struggle for social justice. Those on the margins of society who work to create more just societal and economic structures have in many cases a deep knowledge of God and God's doing that more closely resembles Scripture than do reigning interpretations.

Given the focus on bodies and the importance of communal ritual and ethical practice, Christianity would seem far more at home with an epistemology that honors knowledge gained by the hands than with Descartes's emphasis on knowledge gained only by the head. There have been, from early on and with renewed zeal today, attempts to articulate a Christian epistemology that incorporates body, mind, and spirit, recognizing that human beings know in ways that involve our intellects, bodies, emotions, and wills. However, Christian communities have often embraced other epistemological systems that elevate universal claims aimed at abstract certainty and dismiss, overlook, or even *require* the suffering of bodies. Christians were deeply involved in the trans-Atlantic slave trade, which was partially supported by a Cartesian epistemology that made it easier to imagine that the uneducated slaves laboring in the field were less human than the masters reading books. Christians were also deeply involved in colonization of much of the non-European world, which led to the erasure of peoples and cultures and created regimes of suffering that persist unto the present day. This can be seen in the ways the Bible was used to justify colonialism, leading to the destruction of communities, landscapes, and indigenous bodies of knowledge. In recognition of this history, Christians

must always be self-critical in the construction of new religious epistemologies, asking "who benefits?" and "who suffers?" under any given way of thinking. From racial hatred
to the abuse of power, to religious violence, to economic
inequality, to environmental destruction: all of these have
taken place in the name of Christian faith by those who have
forgotten what faithfully Christian ways of thinking really are.

If it is difficult to discern how we know anything—from hunger to love to geometry—are there particular challenges to
knowing God? Christian traditions say yes.

To put it bluntly, God is seldom obvious. In a world that
contains suffering and meanness, it is not always apparent
that there is a God of love surrounding it all. The most basic
Christian affirmations can seem ludicrous. "Creation is good."
"This world has been redeemed." "God loves you." "Really?"
some might say. "Have you looked out the window? Read
the newspaper lately?" Furthermore, we cannot discover the
intricacies of divinity entirely through careful scientific investigation. This is not simply because our methods of inquiry
are not sufficiently advanced. It is because what we desire to
know—God—is ultimately mysterious and beyond our ken.
Trying to know something of God requires all of our intel-
lect, intuition, and spiritual presence, and still, there is more.
It depends upon the open, attentive heart of the seeker and
upon the self-revelation of God. When it comes to knowing
God, then, Christians rely on revelation. But even revelation, as we have already noted, requires interpretation. Some
forms of Christianity claim that God is fully revealed and so
God has overcome God's own unknowability in Jesus Christ.
But we still need to know what that means. Theologians still
need to work out the fullness of that revelation. Other forms
of Christianity claim that God is still at work in communication, there is yet more revelation, and more every day. "Stay
awake." "God is still speaking." Either way, Christian knowledge of God comes from God's own initiative, which we hold

to be ever present. And human hearts and minds must strive to understand it anew in each generation.

Christian communities describe revelation in various ways. Some believe that all of creation bears the thumbprint of the Creator and that much can be known about God by looking closely at nature. Others have a strong sense of the ongoing revelation of God in the Holy Spirit, who guides and leads people. In general, all Christian communities look to the Bible as a source of knowledge about God, though few agree on how to interpret it. Constructive theology does not see this variety as a weakness in Christian faith, but a strength. In the diversity of interpretations there can remain humility in how much knowledge we can claim for ourselves. Like Mother Teresa we can *know* that the Bible testifies to the God we seek because of the impact of Jesus' story on us and its enduring message of God's love for the world, for each creature, and for us, but at the same time we know that we do not know nearly all of what it contains of God. Our differences in interpretation and in traditions of approach to the Bible keep us awake, alive to possibility, and open to learning.

That is the ideal that constructive theology pursues. We also struggle with the desire for certainty. Especially in turbulent times we must remind ourselves of this ideal when faced—over the Bible—with those with whom we disagree. In much the same way that Descartes looked to geometry and science for universal truth claims untouched by human prejudice or error, some Christian communities look to the Bible for clear statements of universal truth that defy questioning. They turn away from scientific positivism to its mirror opposite, authoritarian religion. However, the Bible is a complex anthology of multiple writings in various genres, composed and compiled over centuries, edited, translated, and interpreted by communities.

Indeed, how communities interpret the Bible is deeply related to the general epistemologies they hold, epistemologies that inform what they are looking for when they open the text. If a given community understands belief as intellectual assent to propositional truth claims, members might read the

Bible to find statements or data. If a given community has an epistemology focused on affections, members might turn to the text to form them in particular patterns of believing, feeling, and acting in the world. Revelation—biblical or otherwise—does not evade the basic epistemological questions.

For multiple reasons, Christian knowing therefore includes *unknowing*. One reason is because the subject matter of religious knowledge is, in traditional theological terminology, infinite. Christians from very early on have affirmed that human beings cannot fully comprehend God, even with revelation. We are finite creatures, with limited perception and understanding. God is infinite and mysterious. The concept of mystery is vital here, for it indicates that our lack of comprehensive knowledge of God is not simply due to our limitations but also due to who God is. Any claim to know God entirely betrays both ignorance and arrogance, as God is beyond what can be exhaustively known. At the same time, to use the argument that God is completely beyond our knowing or understanding can serve as an excuse for not entertaining new ideas from science, or for holding on to cherished, if unjust, notions of God's existence, just as thinking we perfectly know the will of God often excuses wrongheadedness, violence, and cruelty. The question is one of our own accountability. We will discuss this in later chapters, but one way that constructive theology navigates challenges like these is to ask, what parts of what we know or don't know lead to greater love in the world, to the increase of material justice in the world, and to greater flourishing for all? These questions keep us focused on God's love for the world in all of its glory and vulnerability, a world we follow Jesus in loving, passionately.

One form of unknowing in Christian traditions is called *apophasis*, negative theology, or the *via negativa*. This is contrasted to *kataphatic* prayer and theology. Kataphatic prayer might include imagining specific scenes from the Bible, conversing with God directly, or contemplating the attributes of God. Kataphatic theology could include positive descriptions of the Divine. Apophatic prayer, however, would likely include silence, meditation ungoverned by words, and perhaps effort to clear the mind completely. Apophatic theology describes what God is not, negating some of the very affirmations made in other theological moments. This does not only mean simple statements such as "God is not hateful" that paint a positive portrait of God by outlining what God is not. Apophatic theology employs more complicated negations, such as "God is not love." This negation does not imply the opposite (God is unloving or hateful) but rather affirms that even our best human concepts are inadequate to the mystery of God. Theologians and mystics who fall within the tradition of apophatic theology often use contradictory images, such as "shimmering darkness," to break open human knowledge before the God who cannot be comprehended. For example, Pseudo-Dionysius describes the mysteries of God as hidden in "dazzling obscurity," and "outshining all brilliance with the intensity of their darkness.[39]

Another form that Christian unknowing takes is epistemological humility, the posture that we earlier identified as being primary for the work of constructive theology. Knowing that we cannot know everything there is to know about God, Christians have a particular call to be humble in our pronouncements and self-critical regarding our own convictions. We must be attuned to questions of power and self-interest in our accounts of what we know and who has access to knowledge. Given the centrality of embodiment in biblical narratives and Christian liturgies, we must also ask how our claims to religious knowledge affect the bodily well-being of others.

While Christian religious knowledge always involves unknowing, it does not devolve into complete ambiguity or relativity. Christians continue to make strong truth claims with confidence. Some of them are shared by the vast majority of Christians, such as "God is," "creation is good," and "redemption happens." Christians are more divided on other claims, such as precisely what it means to say that "God is Trinity" or "Jesus rose again on the third day." On many pressing top-ics—such as war, sexuality, and other religious traditions—Christians disagree wildly! Within this confusing landscape of unknowing and knowing, humility and confidence, there are some general guidelines to consider.

First, it is important to look at a Christian claim in the context of tradition. Christianity is a conglomerate of long-standing multiple traditions with a great deal of interior diver-sity. This means we have a lot of resources. We have texts, songs, liturgies, artwork, and practices to draw upon. We also have great records of a lot of mistakes, bad arguments, and failed experiments. While people differ on what sources are authoritative and to what degree, part of what it is to be Christian is to know what we know in the context of a long, argumentative, inspired community. Even very recent issues (such as nuclear proliferation) can be informed by this tradi-tion (such as the idea that God created the cosmos is "good"). We face new questions, but we do so in good company.

A second requirement for Christian claims of truth is coher-ence. Here we simply give attention to ensuring that what we say of God, reality, and ourselves makes sense given what we know of the world, what we take as the witness of Scripture, and tradition. By "make sense" we mean that there are not rigid or dogmatic contradictions in our proclamation. Gaps are OK; that is the reality of recognizing unknowing. Willful ignorance, on the other hand, is not OK; it is the exercise of unwarranted privilege that demands obedience.

A third requirement for Christian claims to knowledge is attention to how they affect other persons, creatures, and the creation around us. Truth claims that cause harm to ourselves or others must be questioned and questioned again. Given the most basic Christian beliefs that God exists, creation is good, and God loves us, any claim that fails to promote life must be held suspect.

Within these very broad strokes there is room for much dis-agreement and argument, claims and counterclaims. Diver-sity of opinion is not always an indication of error. Sometimes it testifies to the resilience and flexibility of a tradition, to the strength of a community, and even to the mystery of God.

What significant interlocutors in these matters have in common is that they grapple consistently and honestly with the very questions of knowing and not knowing that are before us, today. Reflecting on their work as our forebears and thinking about what we might appropriate and what we might amend places us alongside others who have sought to know and to be known.

Moving Forward

We turn now to offering some sketches of what epistemology looks like when conjured by constructive theologians. We hope, in this section, to show how we take our own three suggestions seriously, through how we try to learn things by way of skepticism, how we are attentive to dynamics of power and powerlessness, and how we stay in critical conversations with Christian traditions.

Loving the Ruins

Nehemiah was a Jewish servant of the Persian king. When he heard that Jerusalem, the city of his ancestors, lay unguarded and in ruins, he asked his king permission to go and rebuild it. Nehemiah must have loved the ruins he inspected, just before overseeing the rebuilding of Jerusalem's wall. He did, after all, have the thing rebuilt in only fifty-nine days. So the wall that was rebuilt could not possibly have been made of all new materials. With no overnight shipping, new materials of that size and weight would have taken forever to arrive.

Perhaps Nehemiah went out on that first night, before calling his workers to order, to see what materials he had on hand and to imagine what could be done with them. "I think we can use this, and that, and that piece over there," he may have said. Perhaps he discovered certain objects that were just a bit cracked, remembering where they had earlier stood in the beloved city. "We can restore those," he thought. Maybe he saw some things he had always thought were cumbersome but that he realized he could repurpose. "We can use that in a better way," he may have thought.

In any case, before his enemies could even figure out what was happening, Nehemiah had a highly energized team of people working on rebuilding the wall. The team included everyone, it seemed—the text mentions "daughters" who helped in the building alongside "sons," and that "women and children" as well as "men" were included in the dedication ceremony once it was finished. And they all worked quickly and with enthusiasm. Perhaps they, alongside Nehemiah, both loved the ruins and thought they could use them to build something even better, even more life-protecting and life-affirming.

The world is ending as we know it. But there are building materials in the form of everything we have learned all around us. We know some things. We know that we need to unlearn some things. There is knowledge that empires have suppressed and knowledge that doesn't look like science. There are people and animals, plants, and planets with learned and bodily wisdom. The world we want to live in, to have everyone thrive in, is all around us, waiting to be seen, waiting to be built.

Making Space on the Spaceship

Epcot, a park in Walt Disney World, Orlando, features a ride called "Spaceship Earth." It is contained in a big sphere that centers the park. Alongside a partner, you ride in an electric car through the sphere, learning about how, through the ages, human beings have recorded and transmitted knowledge. There are "cave men" (and women!) who write on the walls but then figure out how to write on papyrus and create scrolls that can be transported. Archives begin to be created, protected, destroyed. The alphabet is developed in Egypt. Mathematics, a new discipline, flourishes in Athens.

Artists communicate through painting, sculpting, and making music. The printing press is invented; ideas and news are more widely distributed. Telegraphs, telephones and televisions arrive on scene. A personal computer is developed by Steve Jobs and Steve Wozniak—outside, in a messy corner of a family garage.

What do we do with the epistemology Disney extends to us—and to thousands of riders every year—by way of "Spaceship Earth"? Applying the three suggestions of this chapter, we might begin with the last of the three—being open to what it has to teach us. It is chock-full of information about how we have come to know things, and even more chock-full of optimism about what might be coming in the future (at the end of the ride, in fact, patrons are invited to imagine their own and even better futures).

There is some reason to have optimism about what we will be able to know, and how we will come to know it, and even how accessible it will be to everyone, given the history of how things have proceeded until now.

But applying the first suggestion—that we approach the epistemology presented in "Spaceship Earth" (for example) with skepticism—we have also to ask what is not known that is being left out. What is overknown, presented with too much conviction and too much literalism? And how realistic is it, really, to think that we can construct an even better future? After all, for as much good as ways of knowing have accomplished, haven't they also funded the forces of destruction of life on this planet? How would we go about constructing a better future that is not shaped, primarily, by dominant interests? Finally, if we become overly confident in our imaginings of what is to come, without skeptically remembering that we really don't know, aren't we closing ourselves off to surprise and wonder?

And here the second suggestion made in the chapter comes into play. Appreciating what this Disney ride teaches us, being skeptical about what is left out and what is too certain, how do we then turn to analyzing the power structures and dominant epistemologies in play? Who decides what scenes should be included in the ride? Who decides what should be left out, and at what cost to whom?

It is interesting to note how Disney has altered the ride several times since it opened in 1982. When it opened, an early scene depicted humans conquering the "mammoth beast"—a woolly mammoth. Now, the narration to the scene with the same mammoth emphasizes how human beings learned to communicate in order to survive "a hostile environment." Has Disney become more sensitized to thinking positively about humanity's interaction with other creatures in the world? Initially, there was a scene in which a little boy was surfing the Internet. Later, Disney changed this to include also a little girl. Was this addition due to pressure of feminist and pro-feminist persons who saw the scene as being exclusionary? Or perhaps the pressure came from software developers, who are still trying to figure out how to market effectively to women and girls? Finally, the narration in 1982 ended with the assertion that there were no limits or boundaries to knowledge or possibilities. Today, the final segment includes references to "learning from the past" and "building bridges to others" that were absent thirty years ago. Skepticism might push us to note that Disney might be working harder to be politically correct, given the push, in our globalizing world, for greater inclusivity and the desire for capitalism to expand to the end of the earth. But it would also be possible to credit Disney with learning a better way—using elements of the ruins of this time of endings to build a better, more versatile, reality.

Reading the Bible in the Union Hall

For much of the last two hundred and fifty years biblical scholars have been using the tools of history to try to figure out who Jesus of Nazareth really was. One of the most stringent critiques of this search for the historical Jesus claims that it has too often transformed Jesus into the image of those searching for him. Theologian Albert Schweitzer pointed out over a century ago that, as if looking down a deep well, these scholars have seen in Jesus only reflections of themselves.[40]

Schweitzer's study captured a broad-based agreement that it would not be possible to develop a historical portrait of Jesus. One reason given was the relative scarcity of resources. The other reason, which interests us here, was that it might be a general human tendency to shape things into one's own image. Others felt differently, noting that scholarly objectivity would be able to rescue us from this tendency. This debate continues into the present.

There are, however, other ways of conceiving of these debates that require neither claiming absolute objectivity nor giving in to self-indulgent self-absorption. One of the best ways to figure things out is in the midst of the struggles and tensions of life, where matters often become more real. Union halls are typically places where workers can meet, organize, have educational classes, and socialize. Experiences with reading the Bible in the union hall, bringing together workers and other people of faith, including some theology students and pastors, exemplify what is at stake.

As pressures at work are becoming more and more common, including reductions in salaries and benefits, faster pace of work, fewer rest breaks or none at all, and job insecurity, workers are constantly reminded of their limits. In addition, today's workers are a diverse group, including women, immigrants, and any minority group imaginable. One Bible study group in Dallas includes various groups of workers, including Walmart workers and construction workers. Most of these workers belong to minority groups, which makes them more vulnerable to the pressures of work. Immigrant workers in particular often experience what is called "wage theft," which means that their wages are simply not paid.

Under these conditions, workers hardly feel as though they are in control; as a result, they are not so quick to impose their own presuppositions on others or on a text. Self-absorption is not an option when life is constantly under attack and when personal, communal, and familial well-being are at stake.

In these situations, it is rare that the Bible is read in search of absolute truth claims, for personal self-gratification, or for the sake of learning some interesting facts about the past.

Rather, the Bible is read in search for answers in everyday struggles, which are the struggles of the community. Personal interpretations of what a text says are related to other people's interpretations, and no answer can be considered valid that does not take seriously the pressures and demands of the situation. In the union hall, the workers sometimes deepen one another's understanding, and they invariably challenge the theologians and other people of faith whose readings don't match the reality of their struggle.

Some might argue that such pressures lead to a very utilitarian way of reading the Bible, but they also lead to greater honesty because there is much at stake here, at times even survival and life and death itself. Moreover, it might be argued that many of the texts of the Bible were written precisely in such life-and-death situations of pressure, for the sake of the flourishing and the survival of communities rather than for the sake of narrowly religious or academic reflections. The Bible needs to be read not only in light of everyday life but in the midst of our most existential life-and-death struggles.

Unlike some academics who continue to claim objectivity and some religious people who assume they have access to absolute truth, many of the workers with whom we have read the Bible in the union hall generally have no problem admitting to their own relativity. In this recognition they are being more honest and truthful than those who suggest that a neutral reading of scripture is ever possible. Those workers who are involved in the struggle to make living wages, like the workers from the organization OUR Walmart,[41] know that they have particular interests and needs. They seek practical answers that contribute to the well-being of their families and communities. Common questions encountered in many of these sessions included: How does this reading help me deal with the erosion of dignity and living conditions in labor? How does this reading bring together workers who often share a deep faith but whom the management is actively seeking to divide? How does this reading help us endure the ever-increasing pushback against organizing? Does this reading give us courage to speak the truth?

If the Bible were an abstract piece of writing or a document geared toward only religious individual piety, none of these questions would be appropriate. In the process of reading the Bible in the union hall, however, workers and others who are reading with them are finding new depths in the Bible. Here, we notice that many biblical writings do in fact respond to the questions posed by the workers. The prophets of the Old Testament are also dealing with the lies and distortions of the powerful; the community of the early church is also confronted with pushback by the interests of the religious and political status quo against their organizing efforts; and figures like John the Baptist, Jesus' mother, Mary, and the apostle Paul demonstrate great courage to speak the truth.

Perhaps most surprisingly, the understanding of Jesus also grows when the Bible is read in the union hall. As Jesus was born into a family of construction workers, possibly experiencing the yoke of having to work for large construction enterprises funded by the Roman Empire as well as experiencing unemployment, workers may be able to understand him in ways that tend to escape others. One example is the parable of the Unforgiving Servant in the Gospel of Matthew (18:23–35). In the story, a servant begs forgiveness for a huge debt he owes the king. After the king releases the servant from the debt, the latter turns around and refuses to do the same for another servant who owes him a much smaller amount of money. Unlike many academics and middle-class church-goers, many workers are able to understand that the servant whose debt was forgiven made a mistake when he failed to forgive his fellow servant in turn. Rather than moralizing the story and telling people that they "must forgive" even if they don't feel like it—this seems the common strategy of pastors in established churches—workers understand that the solidarity among workers that is created by forgiveness may be much more valuable than a few bucks.

Embracing relativity, therefore, does not need to end in relativism. Workers who develop fresh interpretations of the Bible and new understandings of the divine are not only speaking to themselves and their own private interests. Union work, understood at a deeper level, is not about narrow self-interest but focuses on the interests of the community—an insight that the unions have sometimes forgotten but are reclaiming these days. As a result, it is not surprising that many working people understand that an injury to one is an injury to all, echoing Paul's realization that if one member of the body of Christ suffers, all suffer together with it (1 Cor. 12:26). What those who are enduring injury and suffering are realizing is relevant to all of us: this "epistemology from the bottom up" is broadening our horizons in surprising ways.

Learning to Breathe in a Buddhist Temple

Death is the ultimate epistemological crisis—for each of us, it's the end of our world as we know it. Of course, everybody knows about death, sort of. But when it comes to this end, there is knowing—and then there is *knowing*.

One of the authors of this chapter, Kathleen Sands, shares her personal story about how she learned this:

> A couple of years ago, I'd been body-boarding in the ocean when a rough wave broke my shoulder. A few weeks later I had surgery to repair the shoulder and a routine chest X-ray revealed that I had lung cancer.
>
> As lung cancer goes, I was very lucky. According to the pathology report, I had only a 29 percent chance of dying within five years. Still, I couldn't help picturing myself in a lineup of three or four people, one of whom would soon be executed at random. The prospect of my own death hit me like a kick in the chest. But it hit me as true. My body knew it to be true. My body recognized death like a gazelle recognizes a lion.
>
> Now, I'm a constructive theologian. So I understand that Descartes was wrong: we are not minds that merely inhabit bodies, but integral body-selves. But evidently this message had not quite gotten through to my own

body-self. It/I was stuck in that lineup with those three or four other bodies, terrified that I might be the one but sick at the thought that anyone else would die "instead of me." Irrational, but definitely how I felt. Certainly, I felt connected—to my own endangered body, to other frail and frightened bodies, to every mortal being. I felt connected, but I did not want to be.

Christianity has many good things to say about bodies and about death. It says that God's own self is embodied—incarnate—which means that God knows all about the shock and crush of death. It promises "the resurrection of the body" and the "communion of saints." It gives us hope, even the expectation, that we will one day see the "face of God." But when death approached me personally, those words sounded like what people say when they want you to stop crying. I did not want words, or images, or "faith" in the sense I used to know. I wanted the feeling of being in the truth, because only that could calm me down.

So, once I'd recovered from surgery, I went up to a Buddhist temple near where I live in O'ahu. The MyuRangSa (Broken Ridge) Temple sits up on a volcanic mountain, so high it seems ready to pitch into the ocean below. It's a steep walk, really a climb, to reach the temple grounds. I pass through a tall gatehouse where a small Buddha sits, guarded by four seated figures, two on each side. They are huge; I see their knees first, then their painted, grimacing faces. A bit of fear, I gather, is the price of entry.

Up more stairs, I enter a verdant courtyard, where a statue of Kuan Yin (a female Bodhisattva) towers among the palms. Around her are the temple buildings, each graceful pagoda painted in intricate designs of red, turquoise, green, cobalt, and yellow. The meditation pagoda is easy to pick out. It's open on one side, and fifty or so people sit on the floor in perfect silence. I step in, choose a spot, sit, and close my eyes. I draw a breath, and then another. A rooster crows. The ceiling fans tick softly. My worried brain goes quiet.

Vipassana meditation is simply breathing. It would be the easiest thing in the world, if we humans knew how to breathe easy. Fretful as we are, though, simply breathing takes practice. And this is how meditation is spoken of: not as a belief system, but as a practice. We begin by drawing deep, gentle breaths. Then we turn attention to each part of the body, noticing and releasing whatever tensions we may find. Finally, we focus simply on the breath as it enters and leaves our bodies. And so we float about, little boats on a sea of air, until the bell calls us back to shore.

Naturally, we have thoughts and feelings as we meditate; the goal is to let them be and let them go. "Mindfulness," the mental state we cultivate in meditation, is like the loving attention one gives to a child. This child may be angry, then sad, and now delighted with this or that; she has a strong opinion, then changes her mind; she is tired, then sleeps, then awakens again. How does one mind this child? Not by going with her every change, but just by staying and watching. This is what makes her feel known. This is what calms her down. And this is how I've found calmness since glimpsing my own end.

Each of us dies alone, but not entirely. Having lost people I loved as much as I love my own life, and having nearly been lost by people who love me that much, I know that in some degree people live and die together. This togetherness, love, is all there is of "answer" to death. Death has called upon me to love the world that was here before me and will live on after me. The end of me, whenever it comes, will not be the end of the world. Death has called upon me to know that this truth is good.

I live on an island that erupted from the ocean floor only a few millennia ago, a moment in geological time. In an infinitesimally smaller moment, that same ocean tossed my life up in the air and gave it back to me. I watch this ocean every day, breathing its long, slow tides, and I wonder whether it watches us, too. Does it see the dogs padding by with their people, the trade-rustled palms, the egret that just now crossed my field of sight? And it dawns on me that mortality, once we know it, is the least lonely of all conditions. Once we know it, though for most of us that's not quite yet. But already and always, we are all like the egret. We are flying through, carried on the wind toward God-knows-where.

Near the end of his life, the theologian Karl Rahner wrote a masterwork called *Foundations of Christian Faith*, that opens with a question with which we want to close our chapter. Rahner wrote,

> [Knowledge] is only a small island in a vast sea that has not been traveled. It is a floating island, and it might be more familiar to us than the sea, but ultimately it is borne by the sea and only because it is [borne by the sea] can we be borne by it. Hence the existential question for the knower is this: Which does he love more, the small island of his so-called knowledge, or the sea of infinite mystery? [42]

This is a tough question to answer, of course. How can we say we love the ocean more than the island when the ocean is primarily inaccessible to us? The island represents what we know: our embodied existence; the resources from our traditions that give us materials with which we critique and create; the practices that shape our days; the stories that locate us and remind us of the meanings we have discovered. To love the island is to love our lives in all their particularities, regardless of how limited they are. It is to value our creaturely existence that is both limited and beautiful.

But how can we say we love the sea any less than the island? The sea is what sustains our particular worlds—even though we don't know the sea in itself, we do know at least this much about it. The sea that is mystery is worthy of our awe and appreciation. Without it, there could be no island to rest on.

We have tried, in this chapter, to suggest ways of knowing both that we are pretty sure about and that lie beyond our understanding. Recognizing the reality of mystery can keep us from speaking with so much certainty that we cut ourselves off from the search for knowledge. When we remember that neither we nor others know all things, we are filled with an epistemological humility that drives us to keep our senses open to how we can learn and know better. Being open to skepticism, as an honest expression of our experience of not knowing for sure, can lead us to learn something new that pushes us to take risks or catches us up in wonder or surprise. Analyzing how power differentials operate in the ways we know the world empowers our determination to pay special attention to what is known by marginalized persons. Drawing from the resources of Christian traditions helps us recognize and value the particular island we are located on, as well as how those who have gone before have honored their relationship to the sea all along. There is a great deal to be learned from our forebears about how to frame and approach epistemological questions, even if we field them differently in our day and age.

We began this chapter by talking about the end of things as they are. Maybe you started these pages convinced, with us, that religious people who forget that their understanding is incomplete are guilty of contributing to the brokenness of the world. Maybe you wonder if any kind of knowledge, any degree of faith, any worthy participation in "religion" is possible, once exhaustive certainty is set to the side for the sake of our world's healing. We think such knowledge *is* possible and worthwhile. And there is always more to wonder about and discover, drawing all and each of us to continue living mindfully, ever seeking to know those things that are most true, just, and beautiful.

Tradition in Action

I n the preceding chapter we explored some of the
ways that processes of knowledge and skepticism
are important to the work of constructive theology
and a life of faith. A significant thread within that discussion
was how we make sense of the wisdom and witness of those
who came before us, even in their imperfections and sometimes grievous errors. For many people, the idea of tradition is
one of comfort and familiarity, of connection to the past and to
community. For others, "tradition" evokes the idea of impris-
onment in backward, superstitious, or xenophobic thinking.
How do we approach the spiritual traditions that have formed
us such that they become neither prisons chaining us to small-
mindedness nor comfort zones so binding that we cannot creatively meet the challenges of our times except by abandoning
those traditions? Constructive theology charts its pathways
between these extremes, recognizing the necessity of understanding where we have come from as a basis for understanding the present and claiming real vision of the future.

In the previous chapter we also discussed the challenge
of knowing in an age of so many different forms of knowledge that—thanks to modern technology, travel, and instant
communication—are intersecting vigorously in new and

interesting ways. Religious traditions are also intersecting in vital new ways. Truth be told, for much of the planet the notion of exclusive tradition and singular religious belonging to one tradition have long been meaningless. For centuries in East Asia, for example, persons have been shaped simultaneously by Confucian, Taoist, Buddhist, and folk religious practices. Even in South Asia, the lines between Christian, Hindu, and Muslim are hard to draw securely and cleanly in local village life since many people understand their lives to involve all of these traditions. Throughout Africa and the Americas indigenous traditions have always existed alongside Christian ones, sometimes harmoniously, sometimes not. And now, what has long been a fact of life outside the West has become a reality for Western Christian theological reflection as well. Because of television and Internet, differences in culture and tradition around the world are more evident at the same time that they overlap and seem more interchangeable.

What, then, does it mean to think about tradition today? We live in a time of ever-deeper awareness of the differences culture makes in what we know. But thanks to the accessibility of information about other traditions, many people no longer neatly stay inside the borderlines of a single religious tradition. Religious traditions have always bumped up against each other and influenced each other. How, then, do we think well about tradition when it finally begins to dawn on us that our religious traditions have never been as singular, unadulterated, and internally homogeneous as we had previously thought? These are vital questions that any rigorous thinking about tradition must face in our time.

The Problems and Possibilities of Tradition

The word "tradition" usually refers to sets of shared meanings and practices that repeat, or have continuity with, the past. Traditions are everywhere. What makes a sports fan part of a tradition? Usually it is a whole array of repeated, shared experiences of belonging with other fans, not to mention special clothing, insignia, and practices on game days or particular slogans and chants about the team (and opponents). Although they evolve, these practices have some recognizable continuity over time, passed down from season to season, senior classmates to freshmen, parents to children. Some traditions are fun, some serve practical purposes, and some are just strange. But the more we look, the more traditions—cultural, familial, political, national, and religious—come into focus. All of them carry certain memories forward and suppress others; they bestow belonging on some, exclusion on others; and they form the basis of social cohesion or, in some cases, like the American Civil Rights movement under the leadership of Dr. Martin Luther King Jr., a means of social change.

Religions don't just have traditions, they *are* traditions. Often in common use, "tradition" is the noun, and the specific religious name is an adjective: Christian tradition, Jewish tradition, Native American tradition. But in the case of religion, and perhaps Christianity in particular, "tradition" is also a very loaded word. As we have already noted in the introduction to this book, some people today consider religious traditions to be the cause of war and suffering, and for them the word "tradition," especially when it is associated with religion, carries with it a sense of the backwardness of prescientific ways of thinking or a blind assent to authority.

Like some of our readers, many of us feel a sense of weight, constraint, binding, and even a sense of guilt about the grave harms the Christian tradition has directly or indirectly inflicted on countless bodies throughout history. The crusades, inquisitions, slavery, and pogroms of the past are repeated in today's global religious conflicts, so for many of us in constructive theology, "tradition" is not a warm and fuzzy word. Under the weight of these associations, on some days, we want nothing to do with tradition.

But can tradition also be a noble word, a healing resource for new life and new ways of being in the world? For most of us, it has always been so. Even as we recognize the damages our religious tradition has inflicted, we have lived by the power and vitality of Christian faith, a faith that does not accept the status quo, that has given us hope. The healing power of tradition is in our marrow; we do not know how to get by without it. We refuse to surrender Christian tradition to those who would deploy it for death-dealing ends. The dynamic multiplicity of Christian communities through time (that is, the tradition) is too rich to have it reduced to televangelist caricature, fundamentalist violence, or stale repetition. We refuse to let toxic uses of the word "Christian" alienate us from that vast two-thousand-year family of stubborn radicals who have always sought human flourishing in the name of the Spirit of Jesus, the one who came so that we might have new and abundant life.

From the tradition of Jesus, we seek new life. But isn't tradition fundamentally about the old? How can it serve the new? Where does the new come from? Out of thin air? Of course not. However counterintuitive it might seem, those who study tradition would argue that the new emerges always and necessarily out of the vast resources of the old, out of a past that is never dead and gone, but a living past that births the new. Although we recognize the dangers and damages of the past, tradition is not wholly vitiated by its wrongs. Despite the damages inflicted in Christian projects of oppression, the Christian past has also sustained oppressed communities—women, slaves, queer folk, and many others—who claimed and reshaped tradition in the name of Jesus who for them is the power of the new. If there is anything unique about the approach of constructive theology to tradition, it is this: we grant privilege to the witness of those who have been hurt and harmed in our world and found faith to be the source of life, over the dictates of those who have been set upon thrones by the workings of religion.

In what follows, we invite you to come with us on a journey to rethink the meaning of tradition in new and creative ways. With fresh eyes, let us look for the power of new life as it bursts into the tradition again and again, leading Christian communities into the future, a future that never simply repeats the past. What if tradition has always been just that— a cumulative project in reinvention, a way of asking what it means to be followers of this man Jesus in every new time and place? Conceived in this way, tradition may well be a helpful companion in these times of endings.

What Is Tradition? A Family Metaphor and Some Key Characteristics

It might be helpful for us to start with an image, a metaphor to guide us through our consideration of tradition. How about the metaphor of the family as a way of thinking about tradition? Families are groups of people joined together by a common history and a common future and shaped by the stories that situate them in a particular time and place. A great-great-grandmother's resilient spirit or a second cousin's secret recipe or a nephew's struggles at his first job are stories that we may have heard over and over. Next year's arrival of a new baby or the endless futures of Thanksgivings to come also form the horizon of our sense of ourselves. The imaginative sense of belonging to a particular family shapes the way we think about our place in the world in relation to others. Similarly, to think of Christian tradition as a family is to name those people at various times and places who have made sense of their place in the world through the story of Jesus of Nazareth. Hearing *that* story over and over, Christians are people in different times and places who have made sense of the world by using the story of Jesus, a story that responds to the deep human experiences of love, alienation, relationship, justice, and the search for meaning.

A question one might ask now is, what is my own relationship to this story of Jesus? Where might I fit in the family of Christian tradition? Do I consider myself among those who identify with the story of Jesus and allow it to shape my life as a member of the Christian community? If I am in this community, do I consider myself one of the guardians of this story, telling it to others in an authoritative way? Or do I see myself among those whose voice has not been heard, as one whose experience is not included in the way the story has been told? Or maybe I have the sense of Jesus as some great-great-great-great-grandparent whose presence within my family may have occurred a long time ago, but since no one tells the story any-more, I don't have any sense of what his life or his good news was all about. I don't really consider myself part of the Chris-tian tradition—I'm "untraditioned." Perhaps I see myself as someone who really appreciates the story of Jesus but is also fundamentally shaped by a different story—perhaps the story of the Buddha or the story of my Native American ancestors. Tradition as a living, dynamic reality might encompass all of these relationships to the family . . . and more.

Stepping back from Christian tradition for a moment, let us think broadly about what religious traditions are in general. Here's a working definition: *religious tradition is the always changing, growing, and contested repertoire of symbols, nar-ratives, myths, teachings, rituals, and other practices (e.g., spiritual disciplines) that a community employs not only to constitute itself as a community but also to orient itself toward ultimate reality and to increase thriving in the community.*[1] In a sense, people belong to a tradition, and that tradition shapes those who understand themselves to belong to it. It is always people who create and shape a tradition of symbols, stories, and practices. The content of tradition is dynamic. Commu-nities are constituted not only by their present repertoire of symbols and practices, and so on, but also by their historically deep, inherited *arguments* about what is and ought to be in their repertoire. How should our stories and symbols be told to best explain how the world works and how we ought to live in it?

Is any old way of telling the story of our tradition or our family as good as any other? No one thinks this. We become a quarrelsome family when we try to decide just how to tell our stories best. Why so much fighting? Because telling and retelling our stories is largely how we decide not just who we have been but also who we are now and will become into the future. Therefore, every tradition struggles with the norms by which it decides how best to tell its story. When we work on making these decisions, we try to articulate and appeal to norms and criteria as ways to give weight to our positions and navigate our debates. Communities also recognize key persons, resources, and moments in their past in which decisions about what it means to be family were made, decisions that they believe should, in some sense, guide all future decision making.

To grasp these dynamics of tradition, let's look closer at Christian communities in particular. Christians usually agree that any way of telling the Christian story must center on the story—the good news—of Jesus. But why focus on him? Jesus was a human being, to be sure, but he was also someone whose way of being in compassionate relationship to others witnessed to a radical love that called others to be human in that way too. Christians very soon after his death and resurrection came to see his way of loving, his way of being Love, as the human face of God. Why make such astounding claims? Because early Christian communities experienced healing and new life in their encounter with Jesus; because discovering him resulted in their re-creation, requiring them to use the word "God" to say that the One whose presence and power they felt in the man Jesus is the same presence and power that created us all in the first place. This conviction eventually led to claims about Jesus contained in the phrases "God become flesh," "Love become incarnate." These are some of the reasons why Christians strive to keep the story of Jesus alive.

Stories are kept alive first by telling them and second by writing and reading them. The Christian Bible has been the most important and consistent resource for making the story of Jesus Christ available throughout the centuries. After Jesus' death, as his following continued, communities that identified themselves as Christian began to share with one another their stories of this man they called the Christ as well as their ideas for continuing to live as he did. The storytelling began. Even in the very earliest period of what later came to be called Christianity, there is variety in the traditions of understanding Jesus. The oldest set of writings we have captures some of these ideas in the form of letters sent from Paul as a leader within and among these communities. A generation later, communities began to put into story form the life and teaching of Jesus and his disciples. These are known as the Gospels and Acts of the Apostles. As the earliest written sources attesting to the life, mission, and death of Jesus, the New Testament as scripture is an authoritative source (in one way or another) for all Christian traditions as they use these writings to continue to tell the story of Jesus in new contexts throughout history and even today. The stories of Jesus collected in the Bible tell us truths about who we are as human beings and about the worlds in which we live. The Bible provides the stories of our being human that are necessary for us as meaning-making beings.

But here we encounter a problem: Christians find themselves in radical conflict about the meaning of Jesus. Inevitably, given the variety of interpretations, we find that we can neither recognize nor believe some versions of telling the Christian story. Indeed, some retellings appear to be neither loving nor healing. How do we decide that some versions of telling the story are so wrong and violating that they must be ruled out as heretical—as impermissible within the Christian family? Think of slave owners' stories of a submissive and obedient Jesus, or Nazi stories about the Aryan Jesus, for example. What are the sources that should count the most as we try to decide what to include and what to exclude? Who gets to decide how the story of Jesus is told? What are the norms by which such decisions are made? We all have convictions that lead us to believe that some ways of telling that story are valid while others are not. For us, the slaveholder's version of Christianity is not equal in authority to the Christianity of the slave who seeks his or her own freedom and dignity in Christ and so does not accept slavery as a natural or God-given condition.

These are all questions about what Christian theologians call *authority*. What is authority? For some Christians, authority names some source, principle, or person (the pope, for example, or a council of bishops) who gets to decide once and for all the answers to these tough questions, something that ends interminable arguments about what it means to be Christian. The authors of this book call ourselves constructive theologians because we are allergic to any account of authority that feels high-handed or authoritarian; we are all-too painfully aware that authoritarians have often violated the marginalized and the impoverished. We prefer to use the word "authority" softly, using the same humility we brought to our questions of knowing and uncertainty in the last chapter. For us, appeals to authority are never meant to silence debate or foreclose conversation. Constructive theologians discover and recognize power and authority in those features of our tradition that confront death-dealing powers, grant life, promote human and planetary flourishing, and lead to justice for all. The story of Jesus and his way of being remains the crucial touchstone in this work.

While Christian communities see themselves as keeping the story of Jesus alive, the diversity of Christian traditions invites us to see that this storytelling (as it becomes theology) is approached with different sources and methods. In being able to tell the remarkable story of Jesus, some communities of Christians follow the rallying cry *sola scriptura* (or Scripture alone) characteristic of the Protestant Reformation and its return to the original sources of the Bible. The best way to tell the story of Jesus is to get as close as we can to the written source—the stories and witnesses to the God-human as they are collected in the Bible. With this approach, some Christians stake the claim that Scripture alone is authoritative.

But is the Bible all we need? For some Christians, the notion that the Bible is all we need feels like an attempt at time travel, a naive desire to bring us into the immediate presence of Jesus and his earliest followers. Because we cannot time-travel, Christians can only access the Christ event—the story and meaning of Jesus—through the resources made available to us and handed on to us through our traditions.

Does that mean that if time travel were possible, we would not need tradition? No. Tradition is also accumulated wisdom—ways in which Christian communities resolved questions about how to follow Jesus in a variety of times and places. Without that wisdom, a wisdom in which many Christians believe divine inspiration and guidance are at work,

Christians would be at a loss in deciding how to be Christian in the present.

Another reason why we cannot rely on the Bible alone is that biblical texts can be confusing sources, given that they were written in different times and places with great internal variety. Many Christians recognize that Scripture is necessarily interpreted by anyone who approaches it. A method in some Christian communities, then, is to prioritize the claim of Scripture with the understanding of *prima scriptura* where Scripture is primary but never stands alone. This emphasis on the Bible as a first point of contact to the tradition of Jesus Christ becomes a cornerstone for Christians who also recognize the importance of interpretation and attention to the complexity of tradition in the midst of an ever-changing world.

We could say that what binds the diverse families of Christians together is that they *do* identify the Bible as authoritative. But diversity also emerges in the way the Bible is approached. Some theological methods insist upon the Bible as a normative source to be placed in conversation with other authorities. In the Roman Catholic tradition, for example, the assertion is that not only Scripture, but also the interpretation of Scripture guided by the teaching office (magisterium) of the church, is authoritative. As the *Catechism of the Catholic Church* states, "'The task of giving an authentic interpretation of the Word of God, whether in its written form or in the form of Tradition, has been entrusted to the living, teaching office of the [Roman Catholic] Church alone. Its authority in this matter is exercised in the name of Jesus Christ.' This means that the task of interpretation has been entrusted to the bishops in communion with the successor of Peter, the Bishop of Rome."[2] In this perspective, Scripture and tradition (understood as the definitive expressions of the community) are equally authoritative, guided by how the teaching office of the magisterium understands them.

In this discussion of the Catholic Church's approach to interpretation and its appeal to the bishops as a magisterium, we come face-to-face with a new sense and meaning of the word "tradition." Now, tradition refers not just to the entire accumulation of Christian history and memory, a purely descriptive notion; the concept of tradition carries a normative sense. Not all that Christians have thought and believed and done is of equal worth. Tradition (with a capital *T*) refers to how various traditions in the Christian family (not just Catholics) try to sort out what is binding for Christians from what is merely accidental or even destructive in the Christian past. In the rest of this chapter, we will try to be clear about small-*t* tradition and big-*T* Tradition in order to distinguish between the descriptive and the normative.

In non-Catholic Christian communities, the quest to determine what counts as Tradition expands beyond a body of authoritative interpreters to include a larger community of participants in the work of interpretation. The source of authority for Anglican (Church of England) communities is threefold: Scripture, tradition, and reason. This means that Anglican Christians agree that they should seek to answer important questions in light of the biblical text but also in light of the long history of Anglican life and teachings. What is more, always and ever careful reasoning should apply. The Wesleyan Methodist pattern is fourfold. Scripture, tradition, experience, and reason are their sources for theological reasoning, adding "experience" to the list because of their deep sense that God speaks through the shared and individual lives of Christians. All Christian communities agree that the Bible as a witness to God's intention and as a record of the first Christians' experiences is constitutive in some way of capital-*T* Tradition. It is the range of diverse methods of approaching the resource of Scripture and the different ways that Christian communities weigh its authority in relation to other resources (like reason or church teachings or individual experience) that expresses the diversity of traditions in Christianity.

Who determines which among the various elements of tradition will be passed on as Tradition? In responding to this question, Christian theologians must be attentive to both the diverse ways in which Christian communities authorize some members to be the guardians and carriers of Tradition and the presumptions about Christian normativity embedded in those authorizing acts. On the one hand, some church bodies emphasize that decisions about the beliefs and practices that are considered authoritative need to be made by specialists who have been highly educated by academic and church experience. For example, some Christian communities understand that bishops have particular authority in determining and interpreting the proper teachings of the church. On the other hand, there are church bodies that understand decisions about authoritative teachings should be entrusted more broadly and more locally, assigning this responsibility to the assembly of believers in a particular congregation (Congregationalists). In addition, many church bodies have particular procedures for voting and election, while other churches rely upon more organic, spontaneous, and charismatic forms of decision making (Pentecostals). Finally, many church communities structure themselves with varying degrees of autonomy and interdependence among their institutional levels: congregational, regional, national, and worldwide communion. Each of these institutional structures comes out of and shapes the understanding and practice of a particular congregation or denomination when it comes to identifying concretely who are the agents that decide which aspects of tradition should be deemed authoritative for contemporary belief and practice. Constructive theologians can be found across a wide variety of Christian denominations, bringing with us different church authorizations and emphases on different sources in theological method. What binds this diverse group together is recognition of the Bible as *an authority among others* and the insistence that new ways of thinking *with* the Bible are necessary as times and contexts change. For us there is no way to bypass the work of critical judgment in the midst of affirming and practicing our many traditions.

Given all of this wonderful diversity in Christianity, how do we decide what in the Tradition brings abundant life? We cannot afford to be naive and say the past is wholly good. We know too much to say that. So how do we sort what is worth saving from what is not? To answer these questions we need norms, criteria that we develop in order to exercise faithful judgment and still allow for the diversity of cultures, histories, and traditions that we bring with us. What are the norms that guide our thought as constructive theologians? While the values enacted by Christians across the centuries have been many, as constructive theologians we stake our claim in a very particular way: We believe that the Christian story must be grounded in the radical egalitarian love disclosed in the life and work of Jesus and his community of followers—love for neighbor, stranger, the poor, the dispossessed, and even the enemy. We pray for the courage and power to resist the forces of violence, racism, terror, and oppression—even unto the cross. We are claimed by an erotic love for the world as God's beautiful creation and so yearn to save it from ecological degradation. These are norms of love, justice, and flourishing. Each one offers substantive guidance. Yet figuring what flourishing, justice, and love should look like in our diverse contexts is a work of discernment and creativity. Christian life is never one thing. We are always learning to be Christian in various times and places. This is partly why we call ourselves *constructive* theologians.

Most importantly, perhaps, all of these norms find their root in multiple passages of Scripture. And they emerge out of a long, resilient history of Christian experience of love in the face of hate, peacemaking in the face of war, resistance in the face of oppression. We understand the norms of flourishing, love, and justice because of centuries of our church traditions of hospitality, proactive refuge, and organizing on behalf of the sick and outcast, of standing up to tyrants big and small. Christianity is full of stories of these norms in action, even in communities that have grown complacent or forgetful—the stories are there, but we have to find and tell them, remind Christians of the Jesus who did these things and the communities who bravely have followed him in love, justice, and flourishing. Finally, we can discern love from hate, flourishing from waste, and justice from oppression because of our ability to reason out the difference between what is life-giving and what is death-dealing on earth. These are the norms we turn to when we affirm a life-giving Christian Tradition. These are the norms that enable us to discern what in the past should stay dead and gone and what must be preserved.

The Ambiguity of Authority
in the Enactment of Tradition

In addition to the diversity of Christian traditions emerging from different approaches to Scripture, Christian traditions have been influenced by a variety of factors, such as geographical locations, social conditions, and wider cultural-religious milieus. Geography, language, culture, and ethnicity have played particularly significant roles, as was the case in the branching of Gentile Christian communities from Jewish Christian communities in the earliest decades of Christian history. The same factors were largely behind the ancient division of the Latin West and the Greek East within the boundaries of the Roman Empire—eventually producing the Roman Catholic and Protestant churches, on the one hand, and the Eastern Orthodox churches, on the other—as well as the proliferation of many forms of Eastern Christianity that eventually came to dot the lands of Syria, Persia, India, Central Asia, and China. Similar dynamics shaped the rise of many denominations and sects within the Protestant family of churches during the last five centuries and the explosion of younger churches in the global East and South today. As Christian traditions spread around the globe, they were shaped as much by geography, culture, and language as they were by their own retelling of the story of Jesus.

Of course, there are still other significant factors conditioning the emergence of diverse Christianities. Take gender, for example. Within any single Christian church, women's perspectives on the content, meaning, and practical implications of the good news, though suppressed and marginalized, have always constituted the voices of "outsiders within." The presence of both slaveholding Christianity and Christianity among the enslaved in the centuries before the Civil War in Christian North America was a searing testimony to the impact of race on how people interpret the gospel.

Talk of gender, race, and slaveholding quickly brings to mind the role of power. Geography, language, culture, ethnicity, gender, and race—and we could add other markers of difference, such as sexuality and class —reveal that our interpretations of the gospel are accompanied by imbalances in power. Unjust power has been most clearly exercised, legitimized, and normalized on the grounds that certain Christians are embodying the right expression of the Christian faith even when their actions cause continuing harm to God's creation and ensure deep regret for future generations of Christians. The most immediate example in North America is the centuries-long Christian tolerance, and in most cases support, of the institution of chattel slavery.

At the advent of European modernity, Christian theology underwent many transformations. One of those included the way in which Christian theology helped to shape the rise of a racialized capitalism, and conversely helped to question it. Max Weber argued in his masterful *The Protestant Ethic and the Spirit of Capitalism* that ascetic Calvinism played an important role in the emergence of the spirit of modern capitalism.[3] As white European businessmen sought profit and began to prosper, Calvinist theologians (dominant in English colonies and in American Puritanism) saw this prosperity as a sign of election by God. The moral contradiction at the heart of capitalism in Europe and in the New World, namely, that *white* prosperity was a sign of election by God, enabled and supported the exploitation and extraction of free labor from enslaved Africans and indigenous populations. The Christian Tradition to which these European Christian colonists appealed in their efforts to expand their wealth through the disenfranchising of native peoples and enslavement of Africans should more properly be called a Western Civilization Tradition than any gospel tradition of love and justice.

This example is particularly poignant because there were Christians involved beyond the slaveholders and their apologists—namely, the slaves! Slave practices of Christianity should have been a big problem for Christian slaveholders and traders, not least because of scriptural claims that in Christ all "men" are free. But the profits were too great and the Christianity that many slaves practiced was glossed as inferior expression of the faith. Although dismissing the humanity of slaves utterly distorted and deformed the integrity of the white slaveholders' own faith and any claim to the gospel story of Jesus, the Christians who profited from slavery willingly destroyed their own faith tradition in order to keep the entire economic and cultural system that supported a global franchise in cotton, sugar, rice, and human lives functioning under the appearance of Christian legitimacy. It is precisely this sort of justification of unjust relations through the distortion of religious traditions that makes the question of who determines religious norms of such interest to constructive theologians.

White Christian profiteers and bystanders were not the only interpreters of Christianity in the emerging North American context. "White man's religion" was regularly and consistently questioned by slaves in the New World. For example, the song "Down by the Riverside" was a counterexpression of slave religion that relocated sacred space away from slaveholding authorities, and it offers us today a new intercultural resource for constructive theology. Black Christian traditions recovered a prophetic character that had been lost to a colonial capitalist modernity. They expressed their Christianity by the use of storytelling in the spirit of resistance, guided by the model of Jesus as cosufferer, the bringer of liberation and resurrection transformation. From abolitionists like Sojourner Truth to theologians like Dr. Martin Luther King Jr., Christians who were excluded from systems of white racial and economic power nevertheless understood themselves called to work for freedom, justice, and peace because of the Christian tradition in which they were raised, not despite it.

Extending the project of justice across racial, religious, and cultural lines, Dr. King advocated a theology of beloved community that he saw as a model for all Christian people. His universalist vision grew out of the Civil Rights movement led by the Black Church, compelled by the momentum of demand for justice that was happening around the world, helped by forces of globalization, such as the African independence movement in Zimbabwe and the antiapartheid movement in South Africa. The prophetic witness of Black Theology in its many forms is one example of the many historic alternatives within Christianity in which our traditions become transformative resources for just practices.

The example of slaveholding Christianity and slave Christianity exposes a profound ambiguity and tension between faithfulness and faithlessness in any genuine talk about tradition. The very etymology of the word "tradition" itself carries this tension: it is related to the notion of "handing over," which implies a kind of transfer over time and at the same time a betrayal.[4] Traditions are "handed over" to new generations and so sustained, but they also have the capacity to "hand over" whole groups of people in the name of tradition. When the Bible is quoted to claim that Africans are descendants of cursed figures, or quoted to keep abused children obedient to abusive parents or battered women obedient to violent spouses, tradition hands them over in betrayal; it is not handed over to them as a way of love and liberation. Conceptual interplays between tradition and betrayal have significance for the work of Christian constructive theology, particularly when thinking about the real lived effects of theological interpretations. Allowing the notions of tradition and treason to interact generates such questions as, Who subverts whom, and how? In what ways do inheritors of tradition betray it, and in what ways do inheritors live it? In what ways does tradition betray its heirs and in what ways does it sustain them? When should subversions be guarded against—and when should they be sought after?

An Explosion of Diversity: Competing
Traditions and the Contest of Authority

Taken together, the multitude of Christian traditions has historically been composed of a few dominant, hegemonic traditions overshadowing many marginalized, suppressed, or simply small traditions. For instance, the power of Western imperialism and colonialism during the last five centuries created the conditions for the current global dominance of Anglo-European Christianities, represented by the Roman Catholic Church and the Protestant/Evangelical churches. Some see the rapid growth of new churches in former colonial domains in the global East and South today as a shift in the center of weight within Christianity from Europe and America to Africa, Latin America, and Asia. Nonetheless, theologically speaking, the newer churches are by and large still shaped in language, symbols, practices, and values by the Anglo-European Christian tradition, which is buttressed by the continued political, economic, and cultural clout of the Euro-American West.

What this all means is that *some* among these varieties of Christianities have come to be viewed as the norm while others, if they appear at all, show up in textbooks, media, and popular imagination as peripheral or even as deviations. Tradition never floats free of other human concerns. Rather it is deeply embedded in material, social, economic, and political landscapes. Recall the metaphor of the family: an extended family might relate tales of its past and its future in someone's home, where the family member with the biggest table and ability to provide the food might guide the direction of the story in a particular way. The result could be that the great influence of material success ends up determining authoritative renderings of the story.

In a similar way, those Christian traditions that come out of contexts of economic, material, social, and political power become better situated to determine authoritative norms. The emperor Constantine in the fourth century CE had enormous material, political, and economic power to make the case for Christianity; his legacy of Christianity connected with systems of power has endured. Joseph Barndt calls this an incarnation of the "Ruler's Church."[5] But there have always been examples of the "People's Church"—those family members in Christianity whose material conditions didn't support authoritative exertions of power but who nonetheless faithfully witnessed to the life-giving power of Jesus. The quiet elder and overlooked cousin at the family table may not have the most material success, but their life's witness and wisdom provide significant claim to authority.

The imbalance in power that has always existed and exists today among the different Christian traditions calls into question any claim made by a single tradition to be the normative Tradition that is supposed to be universally applicable and thus capable of serving as the basis of Christian unity. So when a strongly positioned Christian tradition (small t) boasts of representing the whole Tradition (capital T), it cannot do so authentically. If it claims to know the whole truth of the Bible alone, or to possess the four ancient marks of orthodoxy (unity, universality, holiness, and agreement with the earliest Christian teachings), the theologian may well ask: How is its certainty or unity maintained? What has enabled it to present an appearance of universal, global reach? To whom is "given" the authority to transmit tradition and establish doctrine, thus ensuring its holiness? In answering these questions, constructive theologians keep in view the ways material power may have masked very human, and sometimes unjust, means of asserting and maintaining authority.

To raise these kinds of questions is to unmask the pretensions of any single parochial tradition—regardless of how much material resources and power it possesses—to being the normative Tradition. And this work of unmasking is the first step toward deconstructing the myth of a singular, unadulterated, and internally homogeneous Christian Tradition or Christian identity. The idea of a single Christian Tradition tempts church communities to look for exclusivity or dominance in order to feel authentic. Such myths of purity and exclusivity miss the vibrant reality of Christian faith and are usually based on the suppression of the voices of many traditions with diminished economic, material, social, and political power. Hence, in their work of appreciating the ability of diverse Christian traditions to tell the life-giving story of Jesus ever anew, constructive theologians pay particular attention to those Christian traditions that have been at the margins.

Claiming Justice as a Norm for Christian Tradition

Constructive theologians know that there are many ways of being Christian. However, in our particular time, a time marked by perverse disparities in income equality and the very real threat of ecological suicide, constructive theologians (at least the ones involved in this book) focus on the norm of justice as a way of answering the following question: What are the kinds of beliefs and practices that *should* be passed on into the future, and what should be left behind? Constructive theology thus involves identifying and describing the Christian teachings and the practices that nurture God's promises for justice, peace, and the integrity of creation; it also involves identifying and describing the Christian teachings and practices that undermine these promises. In short, constructive theologians are broadly committed to the idea that material justice is a Christian norm. While recognizing that there are a range of expressions of the tradition, we hold to the idea that faithful expressions of it are ones that engender justice and facilitate Christian ways of being in the world that address the presence of hurt and harm caused by the workings of sin.

This emphasis on material justice has scriptural roots. Justice (*mishpat*) and righteousness (*tsedaqah*) are the Hebrew Bible's most common word pairing (e.g., Jer. 22:3–5; Isa. 28:17–18). *Mishpat* is a multilayered term, embracing both juridical justice enacted in laws and equitable social relations embodied in human beings. While *mishpat* is a foundational conception of justice in the Bible, *tsedaqah* calls the people of Israel to do what is right. We might think of *tsedaqah* as *mishpat* put into practice in the embodied life of the family that identifies itself as "the people of God." It is one thing to

cognitively understand the importance of the concept of justice; it is another thing to put it into practice in our personal
and political lives. This conception of justice drawn from the
Hebrew Bible is not just a matter of personal morality; it also
refers to how all people in the community, especially the marginalized, are treated.[6]

The vision of justice and righteousness expressed in the
Hebrew Bible is evidenced in the life and ministry of Jesus
as he enacted these central elements of his Jewish tradition.
Jesus' own life practice embodied right relation; he embraced
the outcasts and challenged the privileged. As Christians, we
are called to tell this story in such a way that the voiceless and
marginalized are given priority in order to achieve a world of
greater justice and right relations. This posture is one deeply
informed by insights from the fourth-century theologian
Augustine.[7] Expressions of the church exist everywhere that
are profoundly unfaithful in their insistence on bringing harm
to the weak and comfort to the powerful. The task of theology
is to render this unfaithfulness visible while simultaneously
rendering visible the legitimate diversity of its traditions.

Constructive theology requires us to challenge the unspoken assumption that some embody the tradition in an authoritative way simply because of who they are or where they came
from. Almost always this presumption is based on some notion
of cultural or genealogical heredity. This is most apparent in
the North American context of the common assumption that
the tradition of the Christian faith is found most authentically
in the customs and practices of churches that draw a direct
lineage to Europe. Making European and North American
Christianity the measuring stick for all other branches of the
Christian family (bad enough on its own) carries the additional
baggage of presuming the superiority of Western culture—a
presumption that has long undergirded an entire global system of economic and environmental inequity. Put plainly,
white Western expressions of Christianity are presumed to
speak most authoritatively for the Tradition as a whole. It is
just this working of privilege and disadvantage that draws the
focus of constructive theologians to the question of *who* gets

to say what is and is not the Christian Tradition, who and who are not its bearers, and what customs and practices are and are not a part of it.

Does this mean that we should abandon the idea that some expressions of Christianity are more normative, more valid than others? No. It does mean that we should name the diversity of Christian traditions itself as the norm and declare most valid those Christian traditions where love, justice, and flourishing abide. We take our cue from a parable that Jesus told the disciples about heaven, where those who recognized him in life will be blessed. He tells the disciples that in that day the blessed will ask him how they recognized him, and that he will answer that whenever they fed the hungry, clothed the naked, and comforted the sick, they fed, clothed, and comforted him.[8] He did not identify a particular form of religion or a specific orthodox rite. He said he would be wherever and whenever compassionate justice is occurring.

So constructive theologians propose that this compassionate justice happens best when many different expressions of Christian tradition are allowed to flourish, rather than just one. This shift in norms accomplishes several important goals. First, it means that no one ethnic or historically powerful form of Christianity has privileged authority simply because of its cultural dominance or material wealth. Instead, we place diversity itself at the center of any account of the tradition, expanding the horizon of what we mean by the content of tradition. This expansion does more than simply carry on the ancient tradition of seeking unity in diversity. Honoring a diversity of Christian traditions this way helps us see real consequences more clearly when one articulation of the Christian faith holds dominant sway in a particular context. Indeed, it was the absence of such scrutiny that allowed Christian slaveholders to distort their faith to such an extent that they felt no moral compunction to abstain from, resist, or protest against all manner of iniquity against other Christians as well as non-Christians. To the contrary, many felt perfectly able to claim theirs was the true faith even as they engaged in horrific acts of violence and abuse. Had the Christian community as a whole seen the witness of Christians in the enslaved community as a valid and normative expression of Christian faith (rather than an oddity or something marginal), then later generations of Christians would not have been so comfortable with or willfully ignorant of the brutalities of lynching and segregation.

The second helpful thing about seeing Christian diversity as the norm is that it expands our understanding of the "witness of the saints." When we expect that there will be diverse expressions of Christian tradition, we can draw on the creativity and insight of far more sources as we work to understand what it means to be a Christian and to pass that understanding on to our children.

And so, despite the damages some Christian traditions have inflicted, constructive theologians commit to the continuation of Christian traditions out of conviction that love, justice, and flourishing can live strongly within these traditions and nourish new generations of leaders for whom love of the world is a divine call. As teachers and scholars, we make proposals that we intend to follow ourselves, to prepare others to actively continue the ongoing work of Christian tradition *and* to pass it on. Thus, our work participates in doctrinal development and the work of justice, two ongoing tasks of the church. Doctrinal development concerns assessing tradition and appropriating it for the sake of current belief and practice as well as for the sake of future generations. Tradition is not only something inherited from the past. Inheritance has a propulsion toward the future because it becomes incorporated into the legacy that will be bequeathed to Christians who will follow in the tradition. Appropriating tradition involves receiving it as well as assessing it in light of the responsibility to pass on the tradition. These assessments of what is "appropriable" are made for the sake of the future and out of concern for the generations who will follow. In the future's light a twofold responsibility arises. We must allow tradition to question us, subverting our false depictions of the world and overturning our self-reflecting idols so that the voice of God who calls us to respond responsibly through that tradition may be discerned.

Yet we also must question tradition and seek to subvert its mistaken convictions. Both of these responsibilities challenge us because Christian traditions are never simply the voice of God nor are they simply that of flawed and fallen human beings. The Christian traditions offer occasions for God's living word to address the people of the church and call us to recognize our errors in judgment, to repent of the harm we have done as well as turn to new life.

As constructive theologians, we affirm the multiplicity of traditions within our own Christian Tradition, making ourselves receptive to the wisdom of other traditions. But, as constructive theologians deeply influenced by the theological traditions emerging from black, Latin American, feminist, ecological, and queer liberation theories, we see the struggle for material justice as guiding principle for our embrace of the tradition and our interest in passing it on. In continuing these traditions of liberation theory and theology, we see that the colonial legacy of much of the Christian traditions of the West is entangled in a thicket of problems, including white supremacy, patriarchy, and neoliberal capitalism. But we also see that the future of the planet lies in the whole human family pulling together to end poverty and save the earth.

The Multiplicity of Traditions: Christian Tradition in a Complex World

We have now a rich and complex notion of Tradition that grounds our invitation to consider participation in the life of the Christian faith. While all Christian traditions are guided by the story of Jesus, we recognize the diversity of historical, geographical, and cultural locations and power differentials that include race and gender in the diversity of stories told about and with the story of Jesus. At the messy confluence of all of this diversity, constructive Christian theologians propose future-oriented norms of material justice, love, and flourishing to be authoritative as our traditions (in the plural) come together to forge Christian Tradition (as a collective), in the present and toward the future. The norms of material justice, love, and flourishing in the life-giving story of Jesus make it possible to commit to being part of the Christian Tradition, despite the failings in the traditions of the past.

But wait! We have a problem. We now live in a time of forgetting. Some of us know next to nothing about the tradition to which we belong. And some of us no longer think of ourselves as belonging to any tradition at all. We are increasingly unchurched and untraditioned. At the same time, many of us belong to multiple traditions. Raised in religiously mixed families, some of us have to struggle with figuring out what it means when Mom is Christian and Dad is Jewish, or Muslim, Wiccan, or a stalwart atheist. We belong to the age of the hyphen: Buddhist-Christian, Hindu-Christian, Buddhist-Jewish (Bujew), and so on. What does tradition mean for folks like us?

The question of tradition—what the term means and the nature of human belonging to traditions, as well as the possibility of thinking of traditions as families —is complicated in an era marked by global flows, like the flow of information, the flow of mass mediated images, the flow of rituals and practices, and most obviously the flow of persons and communities. Migrations undertaken, willingly and unwillingly, have put persons and communities in unusual and unprecedented proximity to communities and traditions from which they had been widely separated in the past. Geography doesn't quite mean what it used to, and for that matter, neither do our notions of identity, belonging, and tradition itself. These global flows of information and persons have generated a situation in which human beings are routinely working with, dating, partnering with, and marrying people across lines of religious traditions. Families themselves are no longer bound together by a singular religious identity but incorporate diverse religious traditions and their mixing. The notion that a person has but one religious identity generated by belonging to one and only one tradition seems increasingly an artifact of an earlier time in religiously diverse communities. The result is that the very notion of tradition, and what it means to belong to and be shaped by a tradition, is likely to undergo further significant transitions.

These global transformations are hardly matters of indifference to constructive theologians because the theologian qua theologian has long been understood, at least implicitly, to be that idiosyncratic human creature who is uniquely charged with the maintenance, care, transmission, and transformation of a tradition. The philosopher may be a free-ranging bird, but the theologian has traditionally been securely, if often restrictively, housed within the cage/nest of singular tradition, a cage/nest of which the theologian is the custodian.

Constructive theologians recognize that now is not the first time a challenge to tradition has been felt. The pressures of modernity have already served at least partially to dislocate the theologian. After all, Christian theological struggles in modernity and in the wake of modernity have been shaped by the conflict between loyalty to tradition and the critique of tradition in the name of autonomous reason. With the dawning of the Enlightenment or what some call the Age of Reason, Western societies began to witness the gradual erosion—or in some cases, the violent upheaval—of nearly every traditional source of religious and political authority. Events like the Protestant and English Reformations, the invention of the printing press, the emergence of modern science, and the revolutions in France, America, and Haiti prompted the opening of a profound rift between the claims of reason and the claims of revelation.

"Dare to reason" is the Enlightenment cry that for three centuries now has determined how theologians will navigate the question of tradition. To be a modern liberal theologian, one has to find a way of belonging to Christian tradition while dealing with the challenge issued to tradition by the Enlightenment quest to liberate reason from the shackles of external authorities (in church or government) in the name of human freedom and autonomy. This means that Christian theologians today embody the heritage both of Enlightenment reasoning *and* of Christian storytelling. A central question for modern theology has been how to be a thinker of tradition, a thinker invested in the nobility and saving power of tradition, without ceding the reflective autonomy that comes by way of critical reflection. The tradition of Christianity has learned from the traditions of science and reason, but it also has not given up or given over the Christian tradition *to* the reductions of reason and science.

In our new, multireligious situation, the Christian theologian faces not only the challenge of those who would seek to emancipate themselves and others from tradition in the name of freedom—freedom from patriarchy, authority, and dogma. Now, the Christian theologian must learn to think about tradition in the context of the robust, sometimes chaotic, and even occasionally violent encounter of traditions in the plural. The question is no longer one of tradition vs. autonomy, but how to navigate the very *multiplicity* of traditions and the reconsideration of the Enlightenment as itself one tradition among many others.

One way to think about the process of tradition making is as a family reunion in a multireligious and interreligious world. This means expanding our notion of family to include people of other faiths. To begin, the norm of material justice is shared by all three streams of Abrahamic religion. It is proclaimed in the Qur'an, the Tanakh or Hebrew Bible, and the Christian Bible. In the Hebrew Bible (what some Christians call the Old Testament), the prophet Zechariah says, "Do not oppress the widow, the orphan, the alien, or the poor; and do not devise evil in your hearts against one another" (Zech. 7:10). The Qur'an says, "And those who strive in Our (cause),—We will certainly guide them to our Paths: For verily Allah is with those who do right" (29:69, Yusuf Ali translation). And as we already discussed, in Matthew's Gospel Jesus teaches an ethic of the "least of these," calling on God's children to care for the sick, hungry, naked, thirsty, imprisoned, and stranger (Matt. 25:31–46). But this outward-facing vision of human flourishing among members of the human community is shared also beyond the Abrahamic faith families. As John Hick asserts of the many faith traditions of the world, they all teach the ideal of seeking the good of others as much as of oneself.

For example, from Buddhism, "As a mother cares
for her son, all her days, so towards all living things
a man's mind should be all-embracing"; from Hinduism, "One should never do that to another which one
regards as injurious to one's own self. This, in brief,
is the rule of Righteousness"; from Confucianism,
"Do not do to others what you would not like yourself"; from Taoism, the good man "will regard [oth-
ers'] gains as if they were his own, and their losses in
the same way"; from Christianity, "As ye would that
men should do to you, do ye also to them likewise";
from Judaism, "What is hateful to yourself do not do
to your fellow man. This is the whole of the Torah";
and from Islam, "No man is a true believer unless he
desires for his brother that which he desires for himself."[9]

The tradition of atheistic humanism also puts to the fore the
well-being of humanity, even without reference to the theological touchstone of the Christian God. If material justice
and well-being are the norms of our theology, we will find
friends and potential family members among a variety of traditions of the world.

With the norm of material justice in view, we might consider the future of the family as traditions working together
for social change without insulting the integrity of each tradition. We can consider faith-rooted organizing as the expression of faith traditions tapping into their deepest wisdom and
unleashing its transformative possibilities. This type of work
can be shared among people of various faith convictions, as
evidenced in the Basic Human Communities in India (discussed by Michael Amaladoss and Aloysius Pieris) and witnessed in Eboo Patel's Interfaith Youth Core.[10] Faith-rooted
organizing is gathering people to work together for social
change based on the deepest wellsprings of their traditions. It
is shaped and guided by faith principles and practices based
on the belief that many aspects of spirituality, religious traditions, faith practices, and faith communities can contribute in

unique and powerful ways to the creation of just communities and societies. The Living Wage campaign in New York City is one example of an interfaith family working together for economic justice, mobilizing the resources of their religious traditions in a movement for social change through legislation.

In June of 2010 the Micah Institute at New York Theological Seminary began to organize faith leaders in New York City to persuade Speaker Christine C. Quinn and the New York City Council to pass the Fair Wages for New Yorkers Act. Living Wage NYC participated in a silent prayer march to City Hall and mass meetings at several churches, including Convent Avenue Baptist Church, Bethel Baptist Church, and the Riverside Church of New York City. Members of the city council were invited to these meetings so they would see that living wages was an issue that faith leaders across the city cared about and that their communities were committed to the establishment of living wages. Through faith-rooted organizing efforts the Fair Wages for New Yorkers Act, one of the strongest living-wage bills in the United States, became law in June 2012.[11]

One of the primary reasons that this Living Wage NYC campaign was successful was the strength of a citywide clergy coalition that included those from Jewish, Christian, and Muslim communities. This interfaith movement for justice provided a combined moral authority that was greater than the representatives of any one tradition standing alone. This coalition was needed to persuade members of the city council to pass the bill. Instead of using instrumental tactics and power politics to persuade public servants, faith leaders used symbols of faith to inspire them. When the delegation of faith leaders visited with Speaker Quinn's staff in December 2011, they presented symbols of their faith. Rabbi Michael Feinberg presented a menorah, a nine-branched candelabrum used on the Jewish holiday of Hanukkah, and spoke about the meaning of the light of hope. They also gave Quinn a framed photograph of Mother Teresa, a saint in the Catholic struggle for compassionate justice. Since Speaker Quinn is an Irish Catholic, they appealed to Catholic Social Thought, which is the origin of the living-wage movement with the publication of Monsignor John Augustine Ryan's classic *A Living Wage* in 1906.[12] Shortly after this meeting, in January 2012, a deal was negotiated to take the living-wage bill to a vote in the city council.

The Living Wage NYC campaign demonstrates the political possibility of interfaith activism for material justice, an ethic of love, and human flourishing. A coalition of activists successfully worked together in New York City to effect just economic policy change in a city that in recent years had been run like a corporation, without significant regard for the "least of these." The Living Wage NYC campaign became a laboratory for learning for faith leaders who claimed their collective political agency, with a collective power that has the potential to upset and uproot an unjust status quo. This clergy coalition represents a politics of coming to power, living into a wider family of traditions, concerned about justice *for all*, bringing justice to the social structures of political and economic power.

In our world that is characterized by a vast gulf between rich and poor, where consumption has led to environmental degradation, where persons are discriminated against on the basis of their sexual orientations, and where racialized disparities reveal a history of white supremacy, the need for collaborations across religious difference for the transformation of the world is great. If a small group of clergy can mobilize the stories and symbols of their faiths for a change in legislation for greater economic justice, what might the power of our religious traditions around the globe achieve through the transformative possibilities of our stories? How might we work together for social change?

The Future of the Family

The metaphor of the family reunion and traditions as families helps us make sense of the diversity within traditions and the way that the symbols of the Tradition are mobilized to diverse ends. The family metaphor invites us to see, just as we would at a family reunion, that there are differences of opinion within the family and differences of social locations and identities within the family as well. We know that at a family reunion we have both the joyous celebration of time spent together among those with a shared heritage and a shared future and the tensions that emerge among lives so bound to one another. The metaphor of the family reunion might also help us to navigate the new global reality of the flow of cultures and persons, where difference and diversity are no longer contained somewhere else but reside intimately within the family. Through the hyphenated identities of Buddhist-Christians, for example, *other* traditions become part of the family.

Tensions often emerge in the intimate relationships of families because of differing views of what will bring about the family's flourishing, or because of blind spots in personal decisions that affect other members of the family. To be sure, power struggles and dysfunctions are not absent from families. Tensions might also emerge as the result of new family members and friends who show up at the family reunion. The result of family diversity is that there are diverse understandings of how the family's flourishing might play out both collectively and individually.

The metaphor of the family reunion, then, allows us to illuminate the tensions within traditions, not just within the Tradition broadly. Although we might see tensions between the families of Baptist Christians and Methodist Christians, for example, we might also see the tension within the members of each respective family. For within the family of any given tradition of Christianity, there are tensions as the authoritative members of the family claim that their vision and their interpretation is the best, while other members of the family draw from the same family stories to arrive at different conclusions. The metaphor of the family reunion invites us into the tension within the traditions in a playful and evocative way.

Take, for example, the family reunion with particular focus on the Roman Catholic tradition. Perhaps like all those who arrive at this family reunion, members of the Roman Catholic tradition are wearing T-shirts emblazoned with "Put on Christ" (echoing the foundational Scripture of Gal. 3:27), the background of each T-shirt color-coded to a distinct family grouping (the Catholics have green, the Methodists in blue, the Baptists in red). They share the root motto in common, but they have lived it out in distinctive ways. Some of the elders of the Roman Catholic family sit in their circle telling the story of putting on Christ, and as they do it becomes clear that they see Roman Catholic family members putting on Christ in very different ways. All are called to "put on Christ" by emulating Jesus' self-giving care for others, but women are seen as those naturally able to emulate such care in their physicality through their role as mothers. Men emulate Jesus not only through self-giving, but also physically in the biological form of sexed bodies that are able sacramentally to represent Christ as priests. The patriarchs of the tradition have pronounced: In the Roman Catholic tradition of male-only ordination, women are not capable of representing Christ because his body included a penis and theirs do not.[13] Plainly stated, "incarnation of the Word took place according to the male sex."[14] The priest acts in *persona Christi* "taking the role of Christ, to the point of being his very image, when he pronounces the words of consecration."[15] For this group of elders, the exclusivity of a male-only priesthood complements the receptivity of woman as mother in an androcentric church. Such complementarity proposes a family structured by strict gender roles and heteronormativity. While all Christian communities may claim to be "putting on Christ," the interpretation of what this means may be very different.

While the male patriarchs may be putting forth a vision of complementary gender roles for the women and men of the family, at our fictive family reunion there may be other Roman Catholics wearing green shirts telling the family stories in very different ways. Indeed, all of the family may agree that we are called to follow the biblical injunction to "put on Christ," but precisely what this means is envisioned differently by feminist theologians (for example) or Catholic nuns of the Leadership Conference of Women Religious (LCWR). To put on Christ, according to Sister Simone Campbell, is to stand actively on the side of those most marginalized by the economic injustice of late capitalist America. It is to travel to the offices of elected officials to remind them "of the more than 20 million working Americans who earn so little that they still live in poverty."[16] This story of putting on Christ with attention to those on the margins is a story shared also by male patriarchs (see, for example, the US Catholic bishops' pastoral letters on economic justice and immigration, among others). But to put on Christ, for women religious of the LCWR, is also to follow Jesus' vision of God's reign celebrating the dignity of all persons with special attention to women's wholeness and well-being. (This is the central vision of the US Catholic nuns about whom the Vatican claimed that there was a "radical feminist element" and brought the nuns under suspicion for having challenged the patriarchal structure of the Catholic Church in April 2012.) For the Anglican theologian Elizabeth Stuart, to put on Christ means that there is "no longer male nor female" (Gal. 3:28). She quotes the sixteenth-century Roman Catholic Council of Trent to remind us that "in those who are born again, there is nothing that God hates."[17] This allows her to affirm the lives and experiences of gay and lesbian persons as integral members of the family and the Tradition.

This metaphor of a family reunion reminds us that the designated authorities of a patriarchal church are not the only members of the family with access to shared memories, shared symbols, and shared stories. So often in the struggle of feminist and womanist theologians and women in the various Christian traditions dominated by men, the question comes up: *If there is so much on which you disagree with the church authorities, why remain in the church?* It's easy to imagine those at our reunion responding, "This tradition is my family; this is where I find my sisters and my brothers, and my foremothers. The stories that the patriarchs tell are but one of the many sets of stories in our family. We have other stories to tell; the tradition is broader than what the ordained priests, bishops, and other authorities say it is."

By imagining actual persons at our family reunion of Christian traditions we are forced to think about the diversity of Christian traditions not only with doctrines and ideas, but with bodies and the realities of material well-being and justice. Not only are the actual bodies gendered diversely (as in the snapshot above), those bodies have also been racialized. In our metaphorical family reunion we might be forced to ask questions about human well-being, about privilege and dispossession. We might begin to see who is overrepresented and whose voices and experiences are excluded from our conversations or from our circles. The family reunion metaphor replays the concerns raised above about presumed normativity, but it also brings to light in an embodied way how the white, Eurocentric branch of the family has set things up so that they benefit at the expense of Christians (and other persons) of color. Where is the wealth concentrated among the Christian communities and traditions? Why do predominantly white churches tend to be wealthier than predominantly black, Latino, or indigenous churches? The answers may seem obvious on the surface, but it is worth digging more deeply into the real consequences of the ways that power works in the larger church family. "Putting on Christ" in the twenty-first century means putting on the struggles of those in the family and those affected by the Christian family. The metaphor of a family reunion relies on a notion of union, recognizing our belonging *as Christians* in activist organizations in order to affirm our specific commitments to justice, love, and flourishing as Christian commitments, as putting on Christ.

Any family reunion in the twenty-first century should consider the vital possibility that persons within our family may *not* share the same stories. Family traditions that bring in new members—by marriage, adoption, or association—will bring in persons shaped by a different set of stories. The same is true for our metaphor of Christian tradition as a family. The future of Christian tradition may well include the multiplicity of stories that arise from the various heritages of other religious traditions.

The metaphor of the family reunion may also be a useful one for recognizing the ecumenical and interfaith struggles for justice that bind Christians to one another beyond the boundaries of their particular tradition. A constructive theological perspective helps us see that anyone who seeks the material well-being of all is a member of this family. Perhaps at our family reunion, those T-shirted groups are not simply sitting around enjoying one another's company (or not); they are mobilizing for action in the world. They are plotting, planning, and going out to engage in projects for a new and better world of human flourishing that reflects the justice and righteousness of God. Our family reunion might see people of many faiths and convictions joining with others rooted in particular traditions in a common concern for the work of justice in the world, especially among the most marginalized. Dr. Martin Luther King Jr. describes the predicament that we are in as a human family in his essay "The World House":

> Some years ago a famous novelist died. Among his papers was found a list of suggested plots for future stories, the most prominently underscored being this one: "A widely separated family inherits a house in which they have to live together." This is the great new problem of mankind. We have inherited a large "world house" in which we have to live together . . . a family unduly separated in ideas, culture, and interest, who because we can never again live apart, must learn somehow to live with each other in peace.[18]

In this passage King deploys the metaphor of a "world house" to convey the interconnection of the community of creation and the sense that we, as a human family, are all in this together. King challenged the world to seek a deeper understanding of the interrelated dynamics that make up our common life on planet Earth, what globalization theorist Ulrich Beck describes as a "world risk community" where challenges facing the human family are shared globally.[19] Protecting the earth and caring for our neighbors go hand in hand as humanity seeks to live together in peace in a world riddled with violence and conflict. The families of our many traditions must find ways to live together in the one world house.

There are periods in history when humanity is at a crossroads, when the paths that are followed influence large numbers of people in fundamental ways for hundreds of years. We are in one of those periods right now, as the decisions we make over the next decade about the global economy and environment will affect the health and lives of billions of people worldwide for countless generations. Creation is crying out, and we must respond. The poor are crying out, and we must do something to transform the world toward justice. In the twenty-first century, faith communities have a vital role to play in creating communities of transformation committed to economic justice and the preservation of the future of the planet.

If religions are not engaged in the social problems of our times, people will leave them behind as irrelevant and individualist social clubs. Theology must offer an innovative paradigm for Christian traditions to work together and with other religious traditions on behalf of the common good. While respecting tradition-specific ways of engaging the world, theology can offer a horizon of hope for interreligious collaboration for a more just and sustainable world.

Ways of World Making:
Practices of Prophecy and Lament

Introduction

How can Christianity help us to live well in the face of multiple threats to meaning, identity, community, and planetary survival? We see all around us signs of despair and planetary distress, as well as signs of resistance to despair, active protests against oppression, and courage in the face of fear. As we noted in the first chapter, the popularity of the zombie apocalypse genre and the Hunger Games phenomena in popular culture, literature, and film signify many levels of creative disaffection with the status quo—in some cases, shows like these are signs of despair; in others, they are stories of hope that fights against despair, even in extreme situations. This chapter acknowledges the deep-seated worry and sometimes reckless apathy about the future that characterize our day, and it recognizes that too often, religion responds with little more than distractions, condemnations, or irrelevancies. Worse, it sometimes beckons the end. In the face of such realizations, theology's work is to stage a kind of intervention—an interruption of business as usual in order to share a vision of the world that is a different version rooted in life and flourishing. The wager is that this version of things, this constructive Christian theology, is robustly relevant to the questions and challenges we face today. Moreover, this theology can help us live well—that is, with hope, courage, and imagination—in the midst of contemporary threats to meaning, wholeness, and material justice. In fundamental agreement with this basic view of Christian theology Pope Francis has written "The Creator does not abandon us; he never forsakes his loving plan or repents of having created us. Humanity still has the ability to work together in building our common home."[1]

In particular, in this chapter and the next we highlight the concrete *practices* of a life-giving, justice-seeking version of Christianity; a faith to which we have gestured throughout this book. We sketch here a plurality of practices for world making, for remaking the world, in the midst of significant threats to identity, community, and planetary survival. From the cultivation of habits of contemplation and wonder, to rituals of protest and lament, to online community building and to the daily working of the soil, the practices considered in this chapter invite the reader into a capacious Christianity that encourages solidarity and justice. These practices do not deny or suppress the alarming realities of violence toward creation that characterize today's world, but they stubbornly refuse to give these realities the last word, instead calling attention and bearing witness to the resilience and palpable holiness of life.

Zombies as Symbols of What Is Wrong

The dead return with frightening force. Their return within popular culture resurfaces an ancient question: "Can the living be found among the dead?" The walkers in *The Walking Dead*, a record-breaking television series whose protagonists constantly face unimaginable horror and agonizing moral choices, are reminiscent of the biblical figure of the half-crazed visionary standing in the middle of a valley filled with bones.[2] In the ancient biblical text, God poses a question to the prophet Ezekiel: "Can these bones live?" The dead have been dead a long time; the bones are very dry. Before he has a chance to answer, God tells Ezekiel to summon the primal elements, to call out in all directions for the spirit, the wind, the cosmic breath, to bring life back to the valley. Standing in the ruins, Ezekiel hears a rattle. Tendons, muscle, and flesh layer on the bones. It is an ancient vision of re-creation that, while articulated differently, is taken up as well in the book of Revelation.

The current cultural fascination with zombies, robotic alien armies, and post-apocalyptic endgames reaches below the surface, tapping into deep anxieties about the future and global realities that suggest that life is threatened on multiple fronts. Zombies, for example, are a reaction and response to the realities of the present moment. Zombies became proxies, Maureen Dowd notes, "for everything scary that has happened since 2001: 9/11, Iraq, Afghanistan, Katrina, anthrax letters, global warming, global financial meltdown, bird flu, swine flu and SARS."[3] Everyone can add too many items to Dowd's list: the epidemic murders of young black men and women, live-streamed beheadings, the stoning of women, and more. Zombies, vampires, and deadly alien tales pick up these fears and tell a desolating story about multiple threats to human and planetary well-being. They represent a loss of faith in human capacities and an overwhelming sense that no one is really in charge. The popularity of the apocalyptic and the dystopian mediums suggest that they are touching a cultural nerve. What they play out is not the *possibility* of the world's devastation but, strangely, the inevitability and already-occurring actuality of a world coming to an end. The world our grandparents knew is indeed passing, and what is to come is still unclear for all of us. This genre of dystopian horror literature suggests that something is at work within us.[4] It mixes with actual posttraumatic realities, triggering questions about what life will be: Will things and relationships that I care about last? Will I stay connected?

Religion is no stranger to horror, but it contains another wisdom. In contrast to the world-fleeing or world-condemning versions (which religions do also offer), there are versions that can orient us also *to* the world and provide sustaining resources for the world's renewal as we live and experience it. Such religious wisdom can retool us for living amid and through the realities of devastation and scarcity, learning to notice and tend the always present cracks in the pavement of despair, where shoots of green do push through. The question is noticing them and not passing them by as invisible, weak, or insignificant. Constructive theology invites Christians, as well as any and all interested others, into the practice of envisioning and enacting worlds—that is, critiquing and deconstructing oppressive worlds, on the one hand, and noticing, constructing, or creating more liberative alternate worlds, on the other hand. The end, destruction, or de-creation of worlds—through corporate greed, racism, sexism, poverty, war, genocide, and ecocide—calls not for individualism, despair, or escapism but for the constructive creativity of theology as a way of world making, a task done in common, not alone. The anthropologist Margaret Mead is credited with the famous saying "Never doubt that a thoughtful, committed group of citizens can change the world. Indeed, it is the only thing that ever has."[5]

Theology in this vein involves ways of fusing religion and politics to "remake the world" by criticizing the injustices so present in the United States in both our civil and global public life and by actualizing (i.e., imagining and partly incarnating) an alternative, more just, and liberative shared common life.[6] Critically reclaiming and re-creating religious language (found in myths and symbols), rituals, and art can offer a religio-political space for the inbreaking of this alternative world.[7] As Barbara Holmes argues, theology that is being written by some black women today (known as Womanist Theology) embodies "a politics of creativity" that "requires the artistry of humaneness" and "reclaims the past and projects new realities" beyond the interface of racism, sexism, and global economic interests that distort not only black women's lives but all our lives.[8] And yet, making new worlds may also require "spiritual incongruity," or the audacity to reject past religious traditions and political strategies in favor of "creativity in the church and in the public square."[9] As this chapter attests, world making constitutes one way of doing theology, of negotiating among inherited traditions and crafting out of them innovative ways of being and living in our concrete contexts for more liberative purposes, that is, for more humane worlds of meaning and action. World making implies everyday practices that bit by bit remake the world. What we do in our daily lives, in other words, is not neutral to theology, nor to faith. Sustainable food practices, fair labor environments and wages, recycling and investments in renewable energies, protests against cruelty and injustice, and creative, inclusive education are all examples of world making; all are ways of seeing through the ruins of empire to what God's love made—namely, creation in all of its complexity.

The zombie and dystopian films of today confront viewers with questions about how to live on in the midst of tenuous futures. As scenes of destruction spread across our screens, new heroes arise in the midst of hopeless landscapes of mere survival, providing a new moral compass for a shared common life. Figures such as Katniss Everdeen (Hunger Games) and Tris Prior (Divergent) spark a new following, displaying a kind of resilience in the midst of a world that cannot be returned to the way it was.[10] Temple, the main character in the zombie apocalypse novel *The Reapers Are Angels,* demonstrates remarkable inner spiritual strength through all the harrowing trials she faces. These cultural expressions depict despair at unparalleled levels, but they also evoke a new sensibility brought about by different forms of connection and new alliances.

We point to resources for resilience in the face of change even as we recognize that, at times, the experience of the world is overwhelming; global realities seem just too much to bear. The desire to escape is real. We put on our headphones and check out, creating for ourselves a world we can manage. As we present it here, theology both attests to the "too muchness" of our world and yet looks for signs of hope amid the ruins. Such hope is often embodied in very local, very mundane practices. Christian practices are the "things Christian people *do* together over time to address fundamental human needs in response to and in the light of God's active presence for the life of the world."[11] This sounds lofty, but it is not. The things that committed people *do* together over time create ripple effects. Margaret Mead was right—worlds change in small increments, and the point is to tend those increments. Religious people often associate personal and communal identity-shaping practices with rituals that mark major life events, such as birth, marriage, and death. But such practices also include, from the history of Christianity, ascetic, mystical, and spiritual disciplines: forgiveness, healing, hospitality, ministry, celebration, and education. These concrete practices not only establish, mark, and enforce the boundaries of religious or other forms of identity but also disrupt, extend, and chart new existential contours for individual and communal identity. Practices, in other words, can elicit new ways of conceiving our shared common life. Practices also address basic human needs in our broken world, and they can encompass any collective and socially significant action, such as playing, eating and drinking, organizing (for living wages, racial justice, or climate health, for example), parenting, dreaming, caring for elders, and even listening to music.[12] Finally, practices undo any false dualisms between ideas and activities, and thus inseparably connect thinking with doing or, better, they underscore our multiple kinds of doing.

In sum, practices create community in the present across different cultural contexts of Christian life, and across time with past and future Christians. They join religious commitments with real-life concerns that include and transcend Christian communities, and they democratize the doing of theology to include everyday folks and trained experts in their shared task to better the world as God calls Christians to do.[13] Understanding practices as the necessary basis of knowing differently emphasizes "taking part in God's work of creation and new creation."[14]

In a sense, theology runs parallel to creation: it is ongoing, open-ended, and unfinished. At its best, theology also taps into and draws together the liberative dimensions of thinking and doing, of interpretation and action. For example, feminist liberation theologian Dorothee Sölle combined mysticism and political activism to do theology not as explanation or reflection but as in itself communication of an alternative world characterized by peace and justice in contrast to genocide, militarism, and globalization.[15] Likewise, Ada María Isasi-Díaz elaborated *mujerista* theology as a practice in itself, as a critical reflective liberatory act of giving voice to US Latina women's understandings, experiences, and struggles for personhood, subjectivity, and agency amid multilayered destructive forces of racism, sexism, classism, colonialism, xenophobia, and much more.[16]

The practice—the doing—of constructive theology emphasizes and evokes both personal and political dimensions, by which we mean the very real material consequences of theological thinking. It enables persons situated in communities to claim religious subjectivity and agency, "speaking our own word, naming our own reality, reflecting upon and making explicit our own religious understandings and practices."[17] Rather than devolve into identity politics, or a theology of me and mine, it also critiques and denounces those ideological distortions of the Christian traditions that preclude the possibility of a common life in which all flourish.[18] To engage in this personal and political work, constructive theology comprises many genres, "not only linear, logical argumentation but also prophetic denunciation, songs and poems of protest and hope, lamentations, and language of consolation. And our theological language is not only a matter of written words; it includes liturgical rituals, street demonstrations, and protest actions."[19] Constructive theology, then, contributes to cultivating an alternative vision of our sociopolitical order, and in so doing begins to prefigure that alternative vision through life-giving practices. These practices emerge from the vision of life captured by the Christian tradition in the idea of the "*Kindom*" of God.

Wonder

At its best, religion wakes us up. Religious practices can give us eyes to see the world anew and connect to it in deeper ways by leading us to cultivate a sense of wonder. Awakened to the world, we explore what it means to live well in the face of suffering, despair, anxiety, and injustice.

In the Hebrew Scriptures, the sense of wonder at the world is related to "the glory of God," which is represented as ubiquitous in creation. "The whole earth is full of God's glory," proclaims Isaiah (Isa. 6:3); "The heavens are telling the glory of God" (Ps. 19:1). Divine glory is perceived in wind, thunder, and floods: awesome and terrifying. It appears as extraordinary phenomena and most often as the transfiguration of the ordinary—a burning bush, a rock, a cloud. By contrast, the most common images for glory in our culture are starkly different: controlling power, riches and gold, celebrity. Thus, we tend to associate divine glory with might, and we expect to see it in spectacular, extraordinary events. The association of glory with overwhelming power may lead us to lose sight of glory where it is closest to us, where it is most familiar. We may become oblivious to glory when it appears in the subtle luminosity of ordinary things. In order to perceive glory in the ordinary, we need to cultivate the habits of wonder—an enduring attention and responsiveness to the world.

Socrates famously argued, "Philosophy begins in wonder."[20] Wonder has also been claimed as a crucial disposition for theologians. "If anyone should not find himself astonished and filled with wonder when he becomes involved in one way or another with theology," Karl Barth wrote, "he would be well advised to consider once more . . . what is involved in this undertaking."[21] Barth pondered the significance of Socrates's statement, describing a sense of "wonder that is astonished but receptive and desirous to learn."[22] He presumed that the difference between theological and philosophical wonder was that philosophical wonder was only provisional as a point of departure and thus bound to end as soon as the object of wonder was properly understood. In contrast, theological wonder never ends because human beings can never master the "object of theology."[23] Barth seems to be implying that both philosophy and theology begin in wonder, but only theology cultivates wonder because the object of theology, namely, God, can never be completely understood or mastered.

We need not pose such clear oppositions between philosophy and theology or between the ordinary and the divine. To the contrary, the ability to perceive the world as full of divine glory entails overcoming the assumption that we can fully master or possess the world. In relation to the world as in relation to the divine, wonder is *not* merely a step toward mastery, a mere curiosity that is conquered by knowledge. Wonder differs substantially and practically from curiosity. Curiosity is provisional—a passing emotion pursued as a means of instant gratification. As soon as I solve an intellectual riddle or master a new skill, curiosity might end. In contrast, wonder implies both an attitude and an activity of passionate engagement (i.e., compassion) with the beauty and pain, the joy and the suffering, of the world.

Nevertheless, people concerned with social justice are often suspicious of glory. How can we speak of glory, they ask, when the world is so full of injustice and suffering, when so much violence has been perpetrated in the pursuit of glory? We might think that we will be able to perceive real glory *only* when we live in a truly just society. However, we want to suggest that we would not be moved by the suffering of others or have the courage to work for justice if we were not able to perceive the glory in the ordinary things around us.

Some theologies do consider perceiving glory as necessary for a commitment to justice. These theologies recall the words of the early Christian bishop Irenaeus of Lyons: "The glory of God is the human being fully alive."[24] We can sense the spirit of these words in the work of liberation theologians, whose writings express a passion for divine glory perceived in fully alive, flourishing human beings. Latin American liberation theologian Leonardo Boff writes, "Liberation theology recovers the image of God as creator of life, a God whose glory is the 'human being alive.' Among the people for whom death is not a single figure of speech but a daily reality thrust upon them in infant mortality, violent conflict, poverty, and torture, a theology of God as creator and sustainer of life acquires piercing relevance."[25] Likewise, feminist theologian Elizabeth Johnson observes that Irenaeus's statement applies to women as much as men.[26] And in these times of ecological crisis, we cannot limit the statement to the human. In wonder, we connect with the earth itself as a vulnerable site of subtle glory.[27] We do not seek to be attentive to glory because we are distant from adversity. On the contrary, we seek ways to respond to dreadful realities of injustice and cruelty as the very negation of glory. And so, attending to glory wherever it occurs—in the fragile tracks of a tiny beetle, the generosity of a child, or the grand sweep of stars— is an act of justice and love.

The true glory to which the stories of Jesus point does not manifest itself where normally expected, on the side of the mighty, but rather among the weak. It shines in the midst of the excluded, who are denied access to what they need for flourishing. Encountering those who suffer oppression may move us to challenge injustice. Similar to an experience of wonder, this encounter alters perception: we become responsive to a divine element in common reality. Latin American philosopher Enrique Dussel argues, "The cry of pain such as *I am hungry* requires the urgent answer, an answer that issues from a sense of responsibility. . . . It is this responsibility that exemplifies the authentic religion and worship."[28] Conforming to unjust systems—social, political, or even religious—and seeking their promises of might and celebrity may lead us to a sense of tranquility. The cry of the other in pain disrupts such complacencies by revealing the dreadful effects of those systems on the lives of those who suffer from them. Divine glory is seen in a vulnerable human body and in our response to such bodies; it is seen in the threatened earth and in our attempts to relate to it in sustainable ways.

Habits of wonder help us to develop the capacity to perceive God's glory in the ordinary and the fragile—in a burning bush, a passing cloud, or the face of a poor woman. To perceive glory is to awaken to the ordinary, to be exposed to its persistence. This may lead us to joy but also to lament and protest—to lament the violence against marginalized communities and the destruction of the earth, to prophetic protest against the indifference or cruelty that can cause such destruction. Becoming awake to such joy, lament, and protest is an essential form of deep Christian faith.

We see, for example, an awakened sensibility at the heart of the Black Lives Matter movement. People of all ages around the United States express their anger and pain at the persistent violent deaths of people of color—many at the hands of those sworn to protect them—refusing to forget their names and protesting the unjust social structures that have long made such deaths invisible and acceptable. Raising their hands, chanting "I can't breathe," or lying down in die-ins, demonstrators call us to look at the black bodies around us and to see them anew. They seek to disrupt social complacency; they make demands on us, awaken us to the vulnerability and preciousness of all lives but especially to the outrage that particular bodies, black bodies, are historically (and still!) so expendable.

The Black Lives Matter demonstrations remind us of religious rituals of lament and prophetic protest of social negations of divine glory. The protests are both dramatizations and truthful representations of our society. The living bodies lying on the street or the university quadrangle are not the bodies of those who have received the deadliest end of state power. Those bodies are absent. Many of the protesters know that their bodies are overwritten by power, that they are targets for ongoing surveillance and security. Others are simply outraged and consider laying down their bodies as a most appropriate response. They draw our attention to life itself and to the state-sanctioned violence that systematically targets and neglects black and brown bodies. Bringing together embodied gestures and political speech, the cries of pain become impossible to ignore.

Prophetic Protest and Witness

Wonder at the world's beauty and glorious possibilities, combined with anger at injustice and the destruction of life, can give rise to prophetic protest. Jewish and Christian Scriptures have offered Western cultures influential models of this protest. The biblical prophets challenge injustice and reenergize the people by helping them imagine and live out alternative futures.[29]

The force that inspires prophetic vision is recognizable in the context to which it speaks, and yet it is experienced as extraordinary, unexpected, wondrous. The prophets often appear in times of deep despair, when there is a need for a renewal of trust and courage. They may appeal to the righteousness of God, the protector of the weak and exploited who will save, heal, and bring about positive change.

> For you have been a refuge to the poor,
>   a refuge to the needy in their distress,
>   a shelter from the rainstorm and a shade from the heat.
> When the blast of the ruthless was like a winter rainstorm,
>   the noise of aliens like heat in a dry place,
> you subdued the heat with the shade of clouds;
>   the song of the ruthless was stilled.
>
> (Isaiah 25:4–5)

The scope of prophetic commitment can extend beyond the survival of our communities, or even humanity at large, to include all of creation, future generations, species, and life forms. From a prophetic perspective, economic and ecological concerns for justice are intertwined. The whole cosmos is seen as an expression of divine glory. A sense of connection with the world implies reverence and responsibility for present and future generations as well as the planet.

The prophet stands in the valley of dry bones. This powerful image comes from Ezekiel 37:1–14, which describes a time from 593 to 571 BCE when the Jewish people were in exile and an oppressed minority in the ancient Near Eastern empire of Babylon. They lost their land, their independence, even their identity seemed uncertain and thus God seemed far from them; God's power seemed to have abandoned them. This is a vision of disaffection. However, instead of despair in the face of death and destruction, we hear a word of astonishing hope. God demands of the prophet an answer:

"Can these bones live?" Rather than a vision of a valley full of death and dry bones, this is a prophetic vision of life reemerging in unexpected ways. The Jewish people, thought dead and unable to rise ever again, would live to see a new and different future. The prophet sees and speaks about an alternative future. "Thus says the Lord GOD to these bones: I will cause breath to enter you, and you shall live. I will lay sinews on you, and cause flesh to come upon you, and cover you with skin, and put breath in you, and you shall live; and you shall know that I am the LORD." Far from a vision of zombies and the living dead who cannot bring life to anyone, this is exactly the opposite: a vision of defeat turning into something new. The very detritus of defeat becomes the stuff of new life. Impossible, and yet, there it is, over and over again in human history.

Many of the biblical prophets are outspoken and dramatic persons, urging the citizens of the land to change, to cease exploiting the poor, and in many other ways to remember the commitment to social justice rooted in their covenant as a people. Prophets do not celebrate the reigning ideology but rather challenge and protest the present powers. Prophets may push a community to take a hard look at itself or inspire their society to move in a certain direction even though the majority of its members are not yet ready to do so. They may call a group or community to act upon its perhaps forgotten beliefs and realize its best goals. They are often ahead of their time and can be seen as off-center, out of step, and off-key. The very definition of prophetic protest and witness may be to speak, to sing, or to do things that are countercultural or out of step with the masses. Prophetic voices challenge escapism and other means of convenient denial or complicity, pull the veil of denial from our eyes, and force us to face the facts and challenge us to act realistically and hopefully toward transformation, whatever that transformation may look like in our place and time.

In what traditions do we find and recognize prophets today? In the history of US social movements, prophetic protest and witness often entail grassroots, nonviolent, collective action. Such action, says Helene Slessarev-Jamir, confronts the

prevailing unjust sociopolitical status quo while also attempt-
ing to educate about, and partly actualize, an alternative possibility to it.[30] Action such as this edges us and our common
life toward a more inclusive, just, and peace-filled quality of
life. Prophetic work consists of several features. Similar to the
biblical traditions, it taps into theological roots of the dignity,
sacrality, and interrelatedness of all life by appealing to an
equal creation, to divine justice, and to a "vision of hope for
a transformed future in which justice will be realized, right
relations between nations restored, and peace ushered in."[31]
It emphasizes communal rather than individualist or isola-
tionist spiritualities. Prophetic protest may take a pluralistic or multifaith approach to social change. It raises public
awareness about oppression and stands in solidarity with, or
accompanies, marginalized peoples. Such solidarity often
requires relying on and then relinquishing race, gender, class,
sexual orientation, citizenship, or other forms of privilege to
participate with marginalized activists who are challenging
and ultimately undoing that same privilege.[32]

Prophetic protest and witness in its varied features have
manifested in various Christian social justice movements in
the US: abolition, worker rights, antiwar/pacifism, antiracism/
civil rights, antipoverty, feminism, environmentalism, immigrant rights, LGBTQ rights, and prison reform. These movements have contested and critically transformed US public
life, albeit partly, to better embrace and enhance our common life together through "increased political rights, greater
distributive justice, widespread democratization of power,
. . . individual freedoms, and . . . a more compassionate and
rewarding life for the community."[33] Faith-based social justice
movements in and beyond the United States utilize prophetic
praxis to critically disrupt and remake or reconstruct the status quo in light of a more just, more emancipatory future,
often envisioned and pursued in theological terms. Prophetic
protest and witness also carry theopolitical significance when
they mediate present and future realities or "enable activists
to taste the world for which they work."[34] To this end, theologian Mark Lewis Taylor proposes a "Christian theatrics,"

rooted in the prophetic work of US social justice movements. Taylor writes that theater, and the arts more generally, can "unlock an actual world making power in social and political settings. The world that is tasted aesthetically, acted out, especially when done repeatedly, issues in the enactment of new worlds, of new patterns of social and political interaction."[35] Going beyond the performing arts, Taylor's more recent work probes the world-making significance of other creative arts, such as painting, literature, music/song, poetry, sculpture, and textiles.[36] The artful practices of dominated and marginalized peoples carry a "symbolic force" that gives voice to oppressed peoples, who resist and flourish via that art and who "are enabled [by that art] to weigh in to create the world anew."[37] Politically marginalized and minoritized groups mobilize public support and are accompanied by elite empowered groups through this artful prophetic praxis that both dramatizes injustice and attempts to partly actualize an alternative possibility to that injustice via that art.

Spoken Word Art as Prophetic Witness

Today prophecy as public interruption of business as usual can be detected across the globe, bubbling up like so much burning steam from underground pockets of pressure and struggle. It docs not conform to either doctrine or religious confession. Rabbi Abraham Heschel described prophetic speech as volcanic—hot, messy, searing.[38] Another scholar of the Hebrew Bible prophets, Walter Brueggemann, talks of the prophetic vocation as one of poetry.[39] It involves strange juxtapositions—words and ideas slammed together in stark junctures whose tensions occasion something like lightning strikes. One of the places such a public vocation of outraged utterance has emerged with potent force today is spoken word poetry, rendering hip-hop beat and inner-city braggadocio illuminative, probing pain in minimalist expressions of performed language.

For constructive theology, this particular artistry is augury, offering not just insight but also sensation and structure to the subtext of experience. Spoken word makes a world and in that performative space—offered for a momentary hearing—allows for both healing and innovation. Therapeutic enactment of suffering can be coupled with exploratory embodiment of an alternative way of being. In the rhythm and tumble of poetic expression, energies otherwise locked into old patterns are given air to breathe and a template for creative reengagement of life. Annihilation and rebirth are enacted in the same moment of poetic utterance, reflecting the poetic power of Genesis, the first book of the Bible.

Traditionally, many theologians have interpreted the Genesis creation stories as evidence of God's power to create the world ex nihilo, out of nothing. Although there are many ways to interpret the images of divine power resident in those stories, contemporary theologians are faced with relentless global forces of annihilation and so must seek traces of rebirth embedded in even the most complete-seeming destruction.

Typically identified in the Christian tradition as texts of creation ("genesis" translates literally as "beginning," after all), the three different scenarios in the biblical book of Genesis (1:1–2:3; 2:4–4:26; and 6:1–9:28) are better comprehended as texts of *re*-creation. They are each written long after the events described, recording oral storytelling as an act of memorialization, enabling a *re*-genesis to emerge out of an experience of catastrophe. The first, Genesis 1:1–2:3, is probably the latest written and tells of a cosmic creation, where God is less like a person and more like a force, sweeping over "the deep" of chaos and creating light, stars, and earth in seven days. Genesis 2:4–4:26 is older, and tells the story of Adam and Eve in the garden of Eden, explaining suffering in life by their misdeeds and eviction from the garden. Finally Genesis 6:1–9:28 tells of a global flood that kills living creatures on the earth except for Noah's family and the animals he gathers in his divinely engineered ark.

In the long sweep of pulling these various stories into a grand narrative of stories called the Bible, each contributed to a concatenated response to destruction. The garden of Eden tale gave counterpoint to the failure of Israel as a tribal collective, when the fateful choice "to have a king like the nations around" (somewhere around the year 1000 BCE) initiated a four-hundred-year period of oppression, betrayal, and breakup. The cosmic Genesis 1:1–2:3 preface tacked on to the chain of narration as a new beginning actually responded to the exiling of Israel in Babylon after 587 BCE. And the flood story in Genesis 6:1–9:28 remembers an event broader and older than Israel itself, when primal waters took revenge on a world out of control.

Genesis Ex Annihilo

In what follows, Detroit poet-theologian James Perkinson offers a poetic experiment of interweaving such texts of *re-birth* out of *annihilation* into our present scene of global foreboding in the mode of spoken word rhythm. He calls his piece "Genesis Ex Annihilo," or beginning out of destruction. He is acutely aware of the history of American violence, the atrocities embedded in racism, the threat of destruction to planetary life that hovers over us all. For Perkinson, theology must begin in the destruction in order not to re-create it. Read and performed out loud, constructive theology in the mode of spoken word art is not so much *talking about* the possibility of prophetic protest in the art of world making as enacting it imaginatively.

Genesis Ex Annihilo: In the beginning . . . was a catastrophic rupture. A "break" in the music of dawn. The jagged slash of torn flesh, unmended. Followed by desperation, as the tsunamis hit; the lava skyrocketed; night fell at noon. What remained living, fled. Think Viggo Mortensen in *The Road*, the day after annihilation. But the surface was a curve, coming back around on itself; no place to go. Eating became a brief microgenesis in the unrelieved gray, each "found" meal, like a new start, maybe even a new day, until metabolism brought forth its issue. And then the end loomed again, a suffocating blanket of indistinction. Deep black. Deep white. Pulsating, alternating like grammar, like a march nowhere. The beginning of extinction. De-creation.

There have been six such fractures in the flow of time as we know it on this blue marble. We are already racing into this last one, as we breathe, now, in this moment. Is there a creator? Surely! Horrifically, unfathomably, bombastically, it is "us," creating destruction, mirrored on every side in the eyes of those disappearing before our hunger, dodging bulldozers, eating plastic, plankton bodies thinning into mere sieves in the salt plasma. (Imagine watching your blood, your entrails, your breath, exiting your body through your skin, grabbing in panic at each orifice, each bend of a joint, the soft mesh of flesh over your chest, but it all leaks away anyway, as you preside over your own dissemination. *Tohu wabohu*, the Hebrew author calls it.) Two hundred species per day now, going not gentle into that good night. While we press myopic eyes into our texts, grabbing verses, suras, sutras for solace, for a culvert to hide in— like Moses before Yahweh—hoping we come out on the backside of what is passing this way, this "event." But eyes, a billionfold eyes that query relentlessly before they glaze over in oblivion—these relentless disappearing gazes are our bible now. Shall we read one?

Sidney Mead writes of the eclipse of this beginning— a cultivated New Englander of the nineteenth century, traipsing to Oregon, shooting, at a turn in the road, an antelope, and being briefly halted before the quivering body: "When I stood by his side, the antelope turned his expiring eye upward. It was like a beautiful woman's dark and bright. Fortunate that I am in a hurry, thought I, I might be troubled with remorse, if I had time for it."[40] Time—curiously, without time. No end, so no beginning; only Now, Me, the Great Gun-Toting Individual, dreaming "the West," dreaming Hollywood, noting, but unable to be arrested by, the breath-taking eloquence of what was killed for the journey, for food. This is the genesis of America. Charles Long, quoting historian David Noble, plays out the theme: Americans imagining themselves emerging not as sired by what went before, but rather as "children of nature," wombed by a virgin mother, untrammeled earth, redeeming "their ancestors when they stepped out of the shifting sands of European history."[41] The Puritan covenant enshrined in the Jeffersonian republic, leaping forth in grand innocence from the New England forest, like a caesura in time itself! Curiously, surprisingly, America has precisely been an experiment in not having a history. But now the other coast has been reached, the space filled, the planet gutted, and time lurches onto the horizon like a storm. The Now of a coming Apocalypse! Rhizome of Genesis! Up and up, wells the unthought revenge of history. But also this time, the revenge of nature.

So we search the text to ward off the lightning. Forgetting Yahweh began as Baal remade, a storm-deity cascading down a Sinai mountainside in a flash flood of life![42] But that beginning did have its history—slaves escaping the hot furnace of Egypt, a walkout strike from making bricks for cities to house grain for Pharaoh to hoard, stepping forth into wilderness as feral as a Maroon in South Carolina![43] Their exodus was engineered by a Moses of marked transformation—court-raised adoptee, intervening in midlife for his oppressed homies, exiting the empire as an OG,[44] reschooled for a half-life in an outback environment, knowing the Sinai sands like the back of his hand, camping at the base of the heights, ascending like a rod to draw down the electric code of a new community. Lightning strike on rock tablet (or just how do we imagine the commandments' inscription?)! And so it began. But this beginning—as every other we ever remember and re-create in hindsight—needed to birth its own womb, after the fact.

The first Genesis—the Eden-dwelling, tree-tending story—was a later preface to the exodus advent and Sinai decanting of the meaning of that event, once renegade David emerged triumphant over Saul (about 1000 BCE), hijacked Canaanite Jerusalem, and set up scribes to solidify the party line for his throne-taking. Politics adopted—and adapted—its supporting myth. Another four hundred years of power machinations later (cf. 1 Samuel through 2 Kings)—royal hubris to the fore, murders and affairs galore, conspiracy plot upon conspiracy plot unfolding, cuckolding and secession, tax-withholding and rebellion, betrayal, deception, and other such evidence of politics as usual—the beginning had to deal with an abrupt end, in Babylon of exilic fame. Israel was exfoliated as a failed state in 587 BCE, its elite deported, its peasantry hard labored, its memory chanted in prophetic rant, giving rage a vent and making trauma yield meaning in spite of itself. But the nascent experiment in decentralized political decision making and egalitarian land tenure that was Israel's earliest witness—once wrecked in nation-state aspirations—needed a new testament of beginnings.[45] Genesis 1 soon prefaced the older preface (Genesis 2), cantilevering commentary backwards in time, spreading vision to the horizon of the firmament, as dark as the face of the deep before moonrise, as formless as the void, as wild as the wind over Zard Kuh[46] at the height of winter. Here the riff was on the origin myth of their captors, divine hero Marduk and his Babylonian crew, taking the Enuma Elish relished by imperial taste to task, playing the dozens on its mother line.[47] The cut-up body of water goddess Tiamat in that older story is recast, in the Hebrew tale, as the primordial waters over which hovers, mother-eagle-like,[48] the galactic *ruach*, wind-breath of the seven seas, raging gale on Saturn, massive ancestor of every blustering earth-squall like Katrina or Sandy. Genesis has never not been a response to what went before: its commonly held ex nihilo is more accurately an ex annihilo. The beginning grows from a world end. And here in Babylon of the sixth century BCE, the annihilation in question is an *exilio*, beginning again, like the Irish after a famine, or Mexicans post-NAFTA, in a foreign land.

What shall we say of this alternative punctuation of the time of the text? Likely reflected, in that first sagacious tale seeking to give meaning to Israel's new mode of being as a monarchical state in the tenth century BCE, are ancient alterations in our evolutionary trajectory. After multiple hundreds of millennia arcing north out of Africa in tutelage to the perennials of Asia—the original human-grass alliance dependent for its power on the large mammals whose intestines converted the green biomass into meat for us to eat—we began to experiment with a different arrangement.[49] From hunting and gathering, dependent on the flourishing of self-propagating plants and the foraging herbivores and omnivores whose muscles we then metabolized into our own, we turned to an herbal tribe who adopted us into its own sex life. Thus was born our more recent alliance with invasive annuals[50] (oats, wheat, barley, etc.), whose intrusive character we copy, whose soils we prepare, whose seeds we plant, whose competitor-weeds we eliminate, whose fruits we harvest, in the ten-thousand-year-old experiment known as expansionist monocrop agriculture, giving rise eventually to our cities and empires. That changeover was "apocalypse now" for soil communities and ecodiversity alike, wherever it has marched on the face of the planet. And nowhere has it thus far proven sustainable.[51]

Nestled inside this supposedly revolutionary advance from foraging to farming was a Middle Eastern Natufian offshoot at the end of the last ice age—a coupling of humans with trees—fruits and olives and nuts offering sustenance alongside the wild grains.[52] It may well be this brief tenth-millennium dalliance with arboreal cousins that the Eden version of our beginning remembers. But the broad point is that our shift to farming is recalled as "fall" (leading to the archetypal murder of herder Abel by his farmer/city-builder "brother" Cain; Gen. 3:1–4:26). The domestication of plants and animals unleashed a history of calamity for eco-sustainability whose blowback, on a planetary scale, we now stare in the face with trepidation. The planned growth of human-planted grasses has spelled death for the trees—as indeed for an ever-increasing percentage of all the other green-making "mothers" and "fathers" whose offspring we most literally are. The prophet Isaiah had it right: all flesh is, in the most material sense imaginable, grass.[53] But without the flourishing of wild versions of everything, is there hope for the human?

Hope for humans postapocalypse is already a concern in the story of the beginning. In the text that encompasses these two accounts of a necessary reboot—Genesis 2 and then Genesis 1—ecohistory apparently demanded a third (the story of Noah in

Gen. 6). A flood made its force felt, whether relatively local in scale as in the sixth-century BCE breakthrough of the Aegean waters into the Black Sea basin, or in some other more widespread deluge that left scars in memories and traces in myths worldwide. Popular culture today waxes green in the recount by way of Russell Crowe and family riding out the waves of raging divine revolt against human hubris. Noah, in the recent cinematic remix of the biblical tale, assesses the evidence and for love of the environment concludes human experiment and expansion is simply too great a threat to continue. For the sake of everything else, his line of evolution must end. Only the anguish of daughter-love stays his hand. But the agony of his choice was at least made thinkable in the backlash of our hour.

Genesis—our genesis—has raged across the biosphere as a conflagration and disappearance of life-forms now threatening to take down our own house as well. Perhaps the great mercy for the rest of the breathing, keening, chortling, singing, warbling, splashing, digging, winging communities we share the air with would be our own extinction. It will happen. The only question is when. Faithfulness to the wild *ruach* (spirit/ wind) of the beginnings certainly means honoring its roarings and whispers in all the throats and mountains it calls its own. We are but one tiny, tiny word this voice has spoken, and autistic-like and broken, we now labor in terror to sheath our fragility in cyborg dreams of technology, pills and prostheses as our case-hardened facsimile of resurrection. In metal—and meddling—we do trust. It is likely that a new genesis is the coming divine response. The question is: upon whose annihilation will it be built *this* time?

Lament

Lament arises from disaster and loss. As a sustained practice, it can provide impetus for making a new world. Practices of lament decry loss and devastation in affective ways. In so doing, they can lay out possible life-affirming paths, turning grief and anger into commitment, energy, and vision for constructive world making. An example of this is the annual Holocaust Memorial Service at the Congregation Agudas Israel in Saskatoon, Saskatchewan, Canada. Though the Saskatoon Jewish community is small and divided, the synagogue is often full for this service, with many people sitting on stacking metal chairs. A display of photographs and texts lines the side walls, documenting the Nazi persecution of Jewish people that culminated in the Holocaust. The display is the same every year, yet it never fails to shock and disturb.

The service combines Jewish ritual, greetings from civic dignitaries, a report from teenagers on their participation in a Holocaust exposure program, and a speech by a Holocaust survivor. These speeches typically combine humor, sorrow, unanswerable questions, relief and gratitude for survival, lament for those who perished, and a moral imperative: we must act so that such genocide never happens again. The service moves back and forth from the abstract—six million Jews murdered—to the concrete, the specific story of the survivor speaking that year. It moves from prayer and song to address. It highlights but also blurs the distinction between Jew and Gentile. It emphasizes that during the Holocaust, Jews were rounded up and subjected to forced labor and death.[54] Yet other victims are also mentioned. The service is open to all. Every male, regardless of religious affiliation or lack thereof, is given a yarmulke to wear. Prayers are said on behalf of all who died in the Holocaust and other genocides. The speakers address everyone. The service primarily laments the destruction of European Jewry. Yet it evokes, in principle, concern for the well-being of all.

During the service, the mundane and the incomprehensible jostle each other, vying for one's attention. Daily concerns and trivial discomforts occasionally intervene despite the service's overwhelming subject matter. As the speaker tells of horrific suffering and loss, some in the congregation fidget after sitting for an hour on metal chairs. While the solemn liturgy is performed at the front of the sanctuary, the smell of coffee perking at the back conjures up thoughts about the lunch to follow. Some participants, bowing their heads in prayer, worry their yarmulke might fall off. Yet as the service proceeds, this practice of lament reframes daily concerns with a renewed awareness of the fragility of life, the pathos of loss, the privilege of freedom, and the enormity of our responsibility for one another.

The Holocaust has been said to define "inhumanity in our time."[55] Attending this service affirms the value of human life over and against this kind of horror. Lamenting horror can have the unintended effect of making one more human. It prunes one's self-absorption. It renews one's commitment to the world, moving one outward toward others and inward toward God. Lament joins religious emotions (e.g., crying out to God and to one another in prayer about evil and suffering) and ethics (e.g., making God present via our actions). Raising awareness about the suffering of others in this practice of lament can renew and increase shared concerns about human rights.

The service's remembrance and mourning engender a moral imperative for action in the present that will shape the future. Throughout it, there is a constant refrain: this must never happen again. We must commit ourselves to the struggle for dignity and life for all. The prayers and readings, the stories of the survivors, and the photo/text history all combine to influence one's imagination, sense of self, understanding of the world, and place in it. Through this self-reflection and the action it inspires, this practice of lament becomes a way of world making. It can function as a "negative communications"[56] medium, opening one to a broader community of shared concern. It communicates a grave warning: this is what can happen if we do not stand up for the human rights of others, if we do not speak out against prejudice, public scapegoating, and anti-Semitism. At this service, people who might otherwise never meet sit together. They hear each others' voices, see each others' faces, and speak to one another. Some Gentiles wonder what it is like to be Jewish in a world where this kind of horror can occur. Attending the service renews our affective awareness of the Holocaust and other genocides. Lamenting can incite us to solidarity with the victims of oppression and injustice.

As "our understanding grows or decays according to the kind of lives we are leading and the kind of cultural situation we inhabit,"[57] so faith is affected by the sustained practices in which we engage. Lament over the Holocaust (or the victims of 9/11, or the Middle Passage and its spawn of racism, or the tipping of millions each year into deeper poverty) is a cry to God in which protest and intercession combine. If religious faith moves us to attend a service like this one, our faith is in turn challenged and transformed by it, so that the two exist in a dialectical tension. How could this happen? Where is God in the midst of this horror and pain? What does it mean? What are we called to do in light of it? Attending such a service enlivens these questions so that they might shape one's understanding of God and the world. As the practice of lament puts religious faith into dialogue with horrors like the Holocaust, our beliefs take on new meanings. Lament can enliven faith, giving us a renewed sense of the urgency and importance of God. It also complicates faith. As the prayers are said and the readings heard, our hearts cry out to God, "How could you let this happen?" At the same time, many join in the intercessions being made, believing that in the face of so great an evil, only God can give hope. Attending this service makes faith in God more vital but also more tentative. The reflection it gives rise to can reshape Christian claims about divine transcendence and immanence and the limits of human knowing. God's transcendence comes to be seen as a presence that accompanies and sustains suffering people. God's immanence is experienced in their faithfulness and in resistance to evil and suffering.

The systematic theft of Native American lands and cultures,

the Rwandan genocide, the enslavement and oppression of black people—these are only a few of the atrocities that provoke lament. The moral imperative, "never again," arising from lament extends to these and virtually every other crime against humanity and the earth. The practice of lament quickly gathers a crowded agenda, triggering debate over which atrocity gets remembered and publicly recognized. In an unredeemed world, torn by conflicts between peoples and nation-states, lamenting a horror like the Holocaust is never neutral. It evokes concern, in theory, for the well-being and human rights of all. Yet it can also serve to blunt criticism of injustice, in this case of the state of Israel against Palestinians.[58] The constructive theologian, guided by norms of material justice, flourishing, and love, cannot ignore injustice wherever it happens, but doing so does not evacuate the power of lament that can awaken us to "third ways" of healing—where those who suffer on every side of horror are not set against each other but guide us to new pathways of peace, where cycles of violence are named and overcome.[59]

A strange dialectic unfolds as we engage in this kind of communal practice of lament. It exposes us to an event saturated in meaning that continually speaks to us, questioning our faith and making it more vital, renovating our understanding of God and renewing our commitment to justice and peace. We choose to engage in this practice. In turn, it shapes us and our ways of living in the world. Sitting with injustice and decrying it in lament gives rise to a range of ethical practices. The perpetrators of the Holocaust and of slavery denied the humanity of those they murdered and enslaved. Lament recognizes the humanity of these victims, and thus it is a practice of justice toward them. Moreover, it affirms an ancient truth: we are our sister and brother's keepers. We belong to one another regardless of the differences between us.

Ways of World Making:
Practices of Contemplation,
Connection, and Church

Sharing of exercising mercy

Contemplative Practices

To perceive glory, to awaken to the divine power and love embedded in prophetic witness, is to be grasped by wonder. It is to see, often for the first time, or for the first time in a long while, the beauty of the world despite its undeniable horrors and gaping wounds. Such blessed (in)sight, however, can be so fleeting as to seem a phantom or mirage. How can habits of wonder and hearts of compassion be cultivated and sustained?

"And what is a merciful heart? It is the heart's burning for all of creation, for human beings, for birds, for animals, and even for demons. . . . It grows tender and cannot endure hearing or seeing any injury or slight sorrow to anything in creation."[1] Developing a sensibility to glory entails not only an intellectual process but also an affective turn. Contemplative practices can be integrated into faith to generate wonder, compassion, and joy. In such practices, meditation can combine interior transformation with compassionate activity in the world.[2] Contemplation is a feature of many of the world's religions, and the twenty-first century is witnessing a revitalization of this ancient strand of Christian life.[3]

Most religions of the world affirm that the deepest destiny

of humanity is to experience the mystery of reality directly. A Christian contemplative not only *believes* that God is love (1 John 4:8) but longs to *become* love. Or as Marguerite Porete, a thirteenth-century Christian lay contemplative, put it:

> And Divine Love tells me
> That she has entered within me,
> And so can do whatever she wills . . .
> This is the divine seed and Loyal Love.[4]

Because humanity is capable of love, we are called to it; because it is difficult, humanity must practice it. It is difficult to challenge the subtle ways in which love is conflated with preferences for family, friends, allies, religion, race, or nation. Contemplation weakens love's tendency to operate out of the tyranny of egocentrism. Meditation can expose psychic wounds and distortions to divine love to be healed and transformed. Evagrius Ponticus, a fourth-century ascetic, described the birth of love from this healing: "Now this *apatheia* [absence of negative emotions] has a child called *agape* [love] who keeps the door to deep knowledge of the created universe. Finally, to this knowledge succeed theology and the supreme beatitude."[5] As negative emotional habits become less controlling, it becomes more natural to love others. The ego-mind thinks the displacement of the ego by love would be unbearable, but contemplation perceives this displacement as the ultimate happiness (beatitude).

From this perspective, justice is a natural expression of universal love. Abraham Heschel interprets justice as an aspect of God: defacement of creation by human-caused suffering pierces the heart of divine compassion. Prophetic denunciation draws people into the work of justice through participation in the "divine pathos."[6] Through contemplation, a visceral awareness of the interconnection of all beings emerges, which strongly motivates compassionate action. "It is not just a 'logical consequence' that I become involved in the suffering of others, but an unavoidable inner exigency: it is my own pain!"[7] When contemplation and justice are combined, the anguish of this awareness is accompanied by nourishing experiences of divine goodness. This connection between inner transformation and active compassion characterizes much Christian contemplation: medieval women contemplatives' care for the sick, poor, or grieving; the Quakers' antislavery work; and Richard Rohr's Center for Action and Contemplation. Intimacy with divine love deepens compassion, even for enemies. Paul Knitter perceived that the very passion with which he decried injustice generated feelings of self-righteousness and of hostility toward opponents. In his encounter with Buddhist contemplatives, he recognized the crucial role of nonjudgmental compassion for everyone, including those who engaged in destructive acts.[8] Contemplatives, whether Buddhist, Christian, or of other traditions, tend to perceive every being as worthy of care.

Active, universal love is strengthened, perhaps even made possible, through concrete practices that have been refined and reinvigorated throughout the ages by lay and monastic Christians, such as centering prayer, chant, *lectio divina*, silence, watching the mind, compassion, and meditation or intercessory prayer. Mindfulness in gardening, walking or hiking, music, calligraphy, and journaling are also forms of contemplation. Recognizing spiritual friends in other traditions, contemporary Christian contemplatives incorporate practices such as Buddhist meditation techniques, yoga, and Sufi poetry. Contemplation includes periods of meditation as well as the practice of weaving awareness of divine love into everyday experience. Awakening the heart requires attention to the particularity of our own mind as well as participation in what Christians call the body of Christ, that is, all of maimed humanity, nature, and the beautiful, radiant cosmos.

Neither lament nor prophetic work, neither contemplation nor action, neither love nor justice guarantee that species or cultures or the human race itself will be preserved from the destruction we are so energetically courting. The Bhagavad Gita, part of one of the great epics of Hinduism, tells the story of a conversation between the warrior Arjuna and his chariot driver Lord Krishna—who was actually the Hindu deity Vishnu in human form. Standing on the eve of a great battle, Arjuna sorrows over the lives that will be lost—many of them members of his family—by his hand. Like Arjuna on that apocalyptic field of battle, contemporary people may be filled with despair: "Alas, we are about to commit a great evil by killing our own kinsmen, because of our greed for the pleasures of kingship. It would be better if [the enemy] killed me in battle, unarmed and unresisting."[9] If theology is to seek hope, it cannot turn away from the world in despair or assume this or that action will turn the tide. Contemplative practices make the claim that even if individuals cannot control empires, every human being does need to act well, to live with an open and merciful heart, and to respond always to creation's demand for compassion and peace. Contemplation calls its readers to courage and love, even as the zombies approach.

Theology finds witnesses to this kind of hope in the writings of those who have witnessed the end of an age: the Jewish temple bludgeoned to rubble, the Roman Empire brought to naught, the medieval world reduced to ashes. In the teeth of despair, theology turns to the great-hearted ones before us who faced destruction and yet remained faithful to the mysterious ultimacy of goodness. We remember Krishna's words to Arjuna: recognizing both the urgency of action and the dispossession of control, the truly wise "make their lives an unending hymn to my endless love."[10] We sit with Habakkuk by the waters of Babylon: "Though the fig tree does not blossom, and no fruit is on the vines . . . yet I will rejoice in the LORD, I will exult in the God of my salvation. God, the Lord, is my strength; he makes my feet like the feet of a deer, and makes me tread upon the heights" (Hab. 3:17–19). We watch with the medieval mystic Julian of Norwich as defeated soldiers prowl through her city, graves overflow with plague victims, and the church mimics its fantasy of an enraged deity by burning its enemies. We listen as her "courteous Lord" tells her, "Know it well, love was his meaning. Who reveals it to you? Love. What did he reveal to you? Love. Why does he reveal it to you? For love. Remain in this, and you will know more of the same. But you will never know different, without end."[11] The awakening of the heart cannot happen to those who seek an escape from the despairing reality of climate change or remain complacent in the face of human cruelties. Recall Kathleen Sands's story of meditation in a Buddhist temple as she sought to face her own body with cancer. The awakening of the heart, even in the most fearful of life's moments, happens in every act of calming breath, in every act of kindness, in each environmental victory, in the uselessly blooming roadside chicory.

Contemplative practices offer hope not because we can be sure the story will come out happily. Rather, we hope—as we love—because that is the practice of the faithful who are able still to dance because of their faith. Such a dance does not deny the wounds and horrors around us; it does not ignore or repress the very real threats to meaning and community with which we are faced. Rather, it stubbornly chooses life and love in the face of such realities. Contemplative practices can attune our hearts and minds to glory, to the stubborn presence of beauty and of kindness in the thick of the horrors, and those practices can help us to grow beauty and kindness in the thick of things, rather than participate in diminishing them. Awake to the unrelenting biological and moral complexity of the universe, we find we can press on toward hope rather than despair, possibility rather than ennui. With eyes of wonder, the world looks different than before. Challenges and losses that might have been our undoing now appear as invitations to something other than defeat or fear. Ambiguity does not disappear, but now it is the life-giving, justice-seeking possibilities that catch the eye and fuel the imagination. Where before we could see only the foreboding and the fractious, now we become attentive to the openings and connections.

One of religion's gifts can be precisely this shift in vision—the ability to spy out new life amid the rubble, to train our eyes to see not only the suffering that needs protest and lament but also the transformation and healing that could be. For those with eyes to see, zombie apocalypse gives way to beloved community. Out of disaffection and the diminishment of

creation can come life-giving ways of seeing and being in the
world—daily practices that cultivate connection instead of
alienation, wonder instead of fear, courage instead of despair.
Contemplative practices like prayer, silent meditation, singing, and opening oneself to both joy and pain nurture just this
disposition, and over time contemplation's lessons can per-
meate the less rarefied or more mundane activities that mark
our daily lives.

When God Was a Bird: Contemplating
Divine Presence around Us

> But ask the animals, and they will teach you;
>   the birds of the air, and they will tell you;
> ask the plants of the earth, and they will teach you;
>   and the fish of the sea will declare to you
> (Job 12:7–8)

In this chapter, we have begun to argue for the importance of
contemplative practices as forms of world making that affect
both the content and the method of constructive theology.
Theology, in other words, is not only the product of academic
or scholastic rigor. There are myriad forms of contemplation
that temper our tendency toward scholastic arrogance. One
theologian thinks here about cultivating heartfelt compassion
for others and wonder at the beauty of the natural world. A
scholar of religion at a secular college, Professor Mark Wallace was trained to avoid teaching contemplative practices
in the classroom lest students confuse the academic study
of religion with particular sectarian rituals. It is one thing to
study, for example, Christian monasticism as an intellectual
exercise, so the argument runs, but quite another to practice
the daily office as a spiritual exercise. But Professor Wallace
has found that his students are increasingly hungry not only
for religious studies as a detached mode of critical analysis
but also for more experiential learning. He has therefore
begun to use contemplative rituals with students as integral to

their academic inquiries. These exercises affectively ground the analytically discursive work of writing papers and taking exams, and both modes of learning—heartfelt mindfulness and academic analysis—provide the sonic baseline that shapes the rhythms of his pedagogy. He now describes his teaching as a type of soul craft; that is, his intention is not simply to communicate intellectual content but also to promote a form of knowledge acquisition that is grounded in experiential practices. In what follows he describes one such exercise with his students and its effect on him as a theologian:

> I recently encountered a great blue heron while teaching out of doors my Swarthmore College class, Religion and Ecology. I was conducting a three-hour class meeting in the Crum Woods, a scenic watershed adjacent to the Swarthmore campus and near my home where I live with my family. The class began with a silent procession into the woods, where I asked each student to experience being "summoned" by a particular life-form in the forest—blue jay, gray squirrel, red oak, water strider, skunk cabbage, and so on—and then to reimagine ourselves as "becoming" that life-form. After the walk through the woods we gathered in an open meadow, under the shade of a grove of sycamore trees, so that each student and I could "speak" in the first person from the perspective of the individual life-form we had assumed.
>
> I said, "If you imagine yourself, for example, as a brook trout or mourning dove or dragonfly living in and around the Crum Creek, with the creek threatened by suburban storm water runoff, invasive species, and other problems, what would you like to say to this circle of human beings?" This group activity is a variation on a deep ecology, neo-Pagan ritual called A Council of All Beings, in which participants enact a mystical oneness

with the flora and fauna in an area by speaking out in the first person on behalf of the being or place with which they have chosen to identify. A Council of All Beings ritual enables members of the group to speak "as" and "for" other natural beings, inventively feeling what it might be like to be bacterium, bottlenose dolphin, alligator, old-growth forest, or gray wolf. A Council is an exercise in imaginative ontology. Participants creatively metamorphose into this or that animal or plant or natural place and then share a message to the other human persons in the circle. The purpose of a Council, then, is to foster compassion for other life-forms by ritually bridging the differences that separate human beings from the natural world.

On this particular day, as I and my students were imagining and speaking as new life-forms, a great blue heron broke the plane of sky above our heads and glided effortlessly toward the creek. We were spellbound. Flying with its neck bent back in a gentle horizontal S curve, its blue-black wings fully extended, and its long gray legs ramrod straight and trailing behind, the heron darkened the sky above our heads and landed in the shallow water of the creek. Spontaneously, we jumped up from the meadow and walked heron-like—silent, hands held at our sides, strutting in the tall grass— toward this majestic creature now seen stalking and striking its prey with its long yellow bill.

My class and I now felt, it seemed to me, that our imagined metamorphoses had prepared us for a connection—a spiritual connection—to a regal creature whose presence electrified our gathering with agile dignity and rhythmic beauty. We had been discussing, and trying to ritually enact, our identities as fellow and sister members of this forest preserve in communion with the other life-forms found there. But to be graced with the overhead flight and stalking movement of the great blue heron transformed what we had been learning and practicing into a living relationship with a kind of forest deity, if I could be so bold. We stood on the creek bank and watched the heron balance itself on one leg, silently step toward its prey, jerk its bill toward an unsuspecting frog, swallow, and then rise in flight again off the creek, its great wings flapping in unison. Whatever my students' experience of the great blue heron was that day, for me, this encounter underscored my conviction that the Crum Woods is more than a bio-diverse habitat; it is also, in my religious vocabulary, a green sanctuary, a blessed community, a sacred grove, indeed, a holy place.

To call the Crum Woods a sacred grove may seem odd if one is using traditional Christian vocabulary. Histori-cally, Christian theologians avoided ascribing religious value to natural places and living things, restricting terms such as sacred, holy, and blessed to God alone. While the Bible is suffused with images of sacred nature—God formed Adam and Eve from the dust of the ground; called to Moses through a burning bush; spoke through Balaam's donkey; arrested Job's atten-tion in a whirlwind; used a great whale to send Jonah a message; and appeared alternately as a man, a lamb, and a dove throughout the New Testament—Christian-ity evolved into a sky-God religion in which God was seen as an invisible, heavenly being not of the same essence as plants, animals, rivers, and mountains.

But in the earth-centered narrative arc of the biblical stories, this historical devaluation of nature as devoid of sacred worth is entirely absent. In Jesus, God is not an invisible sky God but a fully incarnated being who walks and talks in human form. An astoundingly rich variety of natural phenomena are charged with sacred presence in the biblical accounts, with God appearing alternately in human and plant forms—and animal form. The feathered bird God of creation is the central figure in the Bible's inaugural creation story. In the beginning the earth was formless and empty, and God's Spirit swept across the dark waters of the great oceans. The Hebrew verb used by the authors to describe the Spirit's movement in Genesis 1:1–2 is *merahefet*, alternately translated as to "hover over," "sweep over," "move over," "flutter over," or "tremble over." This verb describes the activity of a mother bird in the care of her young in the nest. One grammatical clue to the meaning of this dynamic verb can be found in Deuteronomy 32:11, where God is said to be a protector of Jacob in a manner akin to the way "an eagle stirs up its nest, and hovers [*merahefet*] over its young." Using the same winged imagery deployed by the author of Deuteronomy, the writer of Genesis characterizes the Spirit as a flying, avian being—a bird or something like a bird—to describe its nurturing care over the great expanse (perhaps we should say the great egg?) of creation. Analogous to a mother eagle brooding over her nest, God's avian Spirit hovering over the face of the watery deep is a divine-animal hybrid that challenges the conventional separation of the divine order and the animal kingdom in much of classical Christian thought.

In the story of Jesus' baptism in the four Gospels, God as Spirit comes down from heaven as a bird and alights on Jesus' newly baptized body (Matt. 3:13–17; Mark 1:9–11; Luke 3:21–22; and John 1:31–34), much as in the Genesis account. All four accounts tell of the same Gospel memory, namely, that as Jesus presents himself to be baptized by John the Baptist, and is baptized, the Spirit descends on Jesus as a dove from heaven, and then, in the Synoptic Gospels, a voice from heaven says, "This is my beloved Son, with whom I am well pleased." In biblical times, doves—in addition to other divinized flora and fauna—figured prominently in the history of Israel as archetypes of God's compassion. Noah sends a dove out after the flood to test whether dry land has appeared (Gen. 8:6–12). Abraham sacrifices a dove to God to honor God's covenant with him to make Israel a great nation (Gen. 15). Solomon calls his beloved "my dove," a heartfelt term of longing and endearment (Song 2:14; 4:1; 5:2; and 6:9). And Jeremiah and Ezekiel refer to doves' swift flight, careful nesting, and plaintive cooing as metaphors for human beings' pursuit of nurture and safety in times of turmoil and distress (Ezek. 7:16; Jer. 48:28). As divine emissary and guardian of sacred order, the dove is a living embodiment of God's protection, healing, and love.

In all four of the Gospel baptism stories, God as Spirit becomes a very specific type of animated physical body: a seed-eating, nest-building, flying member of the avian order of things. The particular beak-and-feathers body that Luke's spirit-animal becomes is defined by the phrase *hos peristeran*, which means "as a dove," "even like a dove," or "just as a dove"—that is, the Spirit's body is thoroughly birdlike. Some English translations of the Lukan and other Gospel accounts of Jesus's baptism miss this point. While the Revised Standard Version says, "The Holy Spirit descended upon him . . . *as* a dove," the New Revised Standard Version prefers, "The Holy Spirit descended upon him . . . *like* a dove" (emphases mine). But the preposition *hos*—from *hos peristeran* in the original Greek text of Luke 3:22 and elsewhere—does not operate here metaphorically or analogically, but predicatively. The phrase "as a dove" (*hos peristeran*) in this context is not a simile that says that the Spirit descended in bodily form like a dove, but rather a depiction of the physical being the Spirit has become. In other words, the Spirit descended in bodily form as a dove. In the grammar of predication, the Spirit is a dove, not like a dove.

Christianity is a religion that celebrates the enfleshment of God in many forms and, in particular, in both human and avian forms. Christianity, in other words, is a religion of double incarnation: God becomes flesh in both humankind and otherkind. My theological point is that as God became human in Jesus, thereby signaling that human beings are the enfleshment of God's presence, so also by becoming avian in the Spirit, God signals that other-than-human beings are the enfleshment of God's presence as well. Christian faith, at its core, centers on belief in God as a fully incarnated reality not only in the humanity of Jesus Christ, but also in the animality, as it were, of the Holy Spirit. If this is the case, is not the wide-ranging world of nonhuman nature—the birds of the air, the fish of the sea, the beasts of the field— the focus of God's interest, not just human well-being? And if this is the case as well, should we not, as human beings, comport ourselves toward the natural world in a loving and protective manner because this world is the fullness of God within the life of every creature?

A theology rooted in the winged God of the Spirit grounds my emotionally felt sense of spiritual belonging with the wider world and motivates me to protect and care for this world. Facilitating my students' ritual work informs my own contemplative practice, which often consists of sitting in a big chair perched at the edge of the Crum forest waiting to catch *my* glimpse of the great blue heron silently prancing along the water's edge looking for a meal. Watching for the heron, I take a break from my mad quest for profit and productivity in much of what I do, and I soulfully drift into a trance state that stills my spirit, calms my body, and fills my heart with joy and wonder at the beauty of creation. In this posture of quiet attention, I meditate on the meaning of Jesus' exhortation in the Sermon on the Mount to "look at the birds of the air; they neither sow nor reap nor gather into barns, and yet your heavenly Father feeds them" (Matt. 6:26). To rekindle my desire to love this sacred earth, I mindfully consider the great blue heron, and all of the other birds and life-forms whom God feeds and supports, in order to remind myself that God cherishes all of us, human and more-than-human alike, and that this is the ground of our hope in a depredated world. So I ask myself, if God was once the nesting, brooding bird God of biblical antiquity, at the dawn of creation and the moment of Jesus' baptism, could not God today be the balletic great blue heron who lives in the Crum Woods? In a world on fire—in our time of global warming, or more accurately, global dying—I wager everything on this hope.

Virtual and Embodied Practices of Hope and Healing

We live in an increasingly digital environment. Many people today bemoan what they see as the alienation and disconnection brought on by what might be called "screen living." The concern is that we are more attentive to our screens than to the real people with whom we live, work, and play in actual time and space. We "like" our "friends'" posts, get our news from 144-character proclamations, and focus our gaze downward as we eat, talk, walk, drive, and commune.

Social critic Malcolm Gladwell suggests that what we create through such behaviors are "weak-tie environments" that become places of escape more than spaces for life-giving connection. According to Gladwell, "The platforms of social media are built around weak ties. Twitter is a way of following (or being followed by) people you may never have met. Facebook is a tool for efficiently managing your acquaintances, for keeping up with people you would not otherwise be able to stay in touch with."[12] Technological advances contribute to the unmaking of former ways of living together, sometimes creating valleys of bones that lie fallow due to lack of meaningful connection.

Since time spent online is a given for billions of people, we need to ask whether or not virtual reality has the capacity to be a strong-tie environment as well as a weak-tie one. What impact could habits of wonder have on our lives as digital beings? Can virtual reality become a space of real depth and connection? Howard Rheingold, author of *The Virtual Community: Homesteading on the Electronic Frontier*, is willing to bet virtual networks can act as strong as "actual" ones. He proposes that "the technology that makes virtual communities possible has the potential to bring enormous leverage to ordinary citizens at relatively little cost—intellectual leverage, social leverage, and most important, political leverage. But the technology will not in itself fulfill that potential; this latent technical power must be used intelligently and deliberatively by an informed population."[13] Attentiveness is key. Preeminent contemporary examples are, as we have noted, the Occupy movement and the Black Lives Matter movement. In each of these cases, social media helped to create the communicative sphere within and around which these movements grew. A theological frame of reference can open our eyes to the destructive functions and impacts of our digital world; it can awaken us to the dangers of superficiality, exploitation, and consumerism that often characterize the digital landscape. In other words, theology can help us see things as they really are and, in so doing, inspire our protest and lament for the world-destroying desires and dynamics that are too often at work in virtual forms. At the same time, however, theology helps us focus on the possibilities for world making that emerge *inside* virtual spaces. With eyes of wonder, we see that virtual reality can become a space for transformative connection and expression. Online communities can facilitate and in themselves enhance our responsibilities for one another, whether through social movements or through caregiving. Since the Arab Spring movements of 2011, journalists, scholars, and others have analyzed the role of the Internet in large-scale movements to envision a more hopeful future. Those movements suggest the possibility of strong-tie environments existing in and through cyberspace. While the debate continues about whether or not the social media–influenced Arab Spring has resulted in more life-affirming societies in that region, theologians understand that cyberspace is changing our conceptions of the world and our place in it. In the work of creating and identifying practices of hope that sustain us, then, we need to attend to how the Internet both inhibits *and opens up* space where hope can be nurtured.

Web sites like CaringBridge, which is dedicated to connecting people with serious illnesses or injuries with those who care about them, create communities that can be profoundly healing.[14] Journal entries sent out by those living through chemotherapy and hospitalization inspire followers to post messages of support in return. Even though sites like CaringBridge are intended to be a tool to keep others updated on developments of those living with life-threatening conditions, they often evolve into much more. Health updates start conversations with assemblies of people who respond with stories of their own navigation of similar health journeys, with prayers and support, and with concrete acts of care for those who share their journeys in this way. These virtual connections do much to sustain those suffering through the dry-boned valley of cancer and other serious conditions. Just seeing the prayers written by far-flung others (or having them read at one's bedside) in the midst of grave illness is a form of medicine, a deep connective help

in a time of fear and loneliness. It can be a profound movement of Spirit.

At the same time, publicly narrating an illness or injury
for hundreds to read and to comment on is a risky venture.
Moral philosopher Annette Baier suggests that "where one
depends on another's good will, one is necessarily vulnerable
to the limits of that good will. One leaves others an opportunity to harm one when one trusts, and also shows one's confidence that they will not take it."[15] Similar to other forms
of communication, there will be responses posted online
that those living with serious illness or injury find less than
helpful. Given their popularity, however, users of sites like
CaringBridge seem to find support and sustenance, even as
cancer and other illnesses threaten to destroy connections,
faith, and hope.

Theological language and concepts can illuminate such
experiences. One of the most prominent biblical images for
the church is the body of Christ, an image used not only to
refer to local Christian communities but also to portray what
Christians have long confessed to be the "church universal."[16] If members of this body actually represent Christ in
the world, then, they—we—are called to do as Christ did: to
be with people during their darkest hours, to offer hope and
healing, to let them know that illness and death do not have
the last word.[17] Given the life-giving and even salvific experiences that those living with serious illnesses have had with
online communities like CaringBridge, theologians might
describe such communities as manifestations of the *virtual*
body of Christ.

To pose such a possibility is not to place less emphasis on
the *actual* body of Christ present in concrete, particular, local
communities. Yet in a world where our wired lives increasingly *are* our lives, we must pay vital attention not only to
forms of disconnect fostered by technology but also to re-
creations of *virtual* communities of hope. Journalist Margaret
Wertheim proposes that "our common task [is] to do better
with the Net than we have done with the physical world."[18]
Even as we generate examples of how the Internet enables

people to behave more poorly online than they do in person, we note that at times cyberspace allows us to do better than we do in person. For instance, many of us know that we can share our grief or sadness more easily in online posts than in face-to-face conversations, especially if we are traumatized by cancer or other serious diagnoses. In virtual reality, tears do not make words unintelligible. With online posts, we can go back and edit some sentences that sound more bitter than we intended or prefer. In cyberspace, our vulnerabilities can at times be better managed than in face-to-face interactions. Also, being clearer about how we are doing often enables others to be clearer about how to be supportive. In all these instances, we find conditions for the possibility of the body of Christ to materialize made manifest in life-giving *virtual* ways.

Thinking about sites like CaringBridge as becoming the virtual body of Christ is complicated by the fact that the boundaries of online communities are generally more porous than our physical communities. So the virtual body of Christ can (and often does) include people who do not identify as Christian. Can such a religiously diverse community still be called "the body of Christ" without falling prey to Christian supremacy, that is, interpreting other religions through Christian lenses rather than on their own terms?[19] Theologian Deanna Thompson lives with stage IV cancer and uses that experience to think theologically about the body of Christ:

> I've become convinced that the church universal extends even further, beyond the bounds of Christian communities to include those of other faiths and even those of no particular faith. Take the grace bestowed upon me by one of my agnostic Jewish colleagues. Shortly after she returned from a trip to Israel, this Jewish colleague sent me an email about how my postings on CaringBridge had become a source of inspiration to her. Spurred on by my story, she had even gone out on a limb and attempted to pray herself. My colleague then went on to describe her visits

to several churches in Israel, and how in each one she
had knelt and prayed, asking Jesus for a favor, that he
might heal her friend with cancer.[20]

That an agnostic Jew would kneel in churches throughout Israel to pray for her Christian friend living with cancer
suggests that *virtual* connections can and do become sites of
hope and that the Internet is capable of facilitating strong-
tie environments where grace is given and embraces are felt
in bodily ways. New levels of relationships that form in part
through contact via sites like CaringBridge tug at the boundaries and limits of theological understandings and practices of
who constitutes the body of Christ. Christians suffering from
cancer are prayed for by Jews and Hindus, are blessed by
Native American blessings, and serve as the focus of Buddhist
meditation sessions,[21] all of which calls for fresh theological
views and practices regarding what medieval Christian mystic
Teresa of Avila describes in her poem "Christ Has No Body":
"Christ has no body but yours / No hands, no feet on earth but
yours."[22] Multireligious prayers for healing in and beyond an
online community broaden Christian theological notions of
the church as the body of Christ, in which our identities, ways
of life, and well-being are inextricably interconnected to a
cloud of witnesses not only across time, space, and materiality
but also across religious traditions. With respect to the body
of Christ and the church universal, then, communities of support created via the Internet encourage us to think beyond
conventional categories and practices of who and what count
as church, to think about what new possibilities of re-creation
are made possible by what we are calling the *virtual* body of
Christ.

Local communities of faith surely continue to embody
divine healing and hopeful presence for those who suffer. Yet
recent experiences with virtual communities also show us that
the kind of hope we so desperately need will often include
cyberspace. Theology highlights the ways in which the Internet shapes current practices of hope and movements of healing or prophetic spirit, and its cultivation of wonder puts us

on the lookout for potentially unlikely and oftentimes surprising ways that cyberspace becomes a vital space for increasing material justice, love, and flourishing.

Even as we become increasingly digital creatures, many people also reach for what we might call incarnational practices: ways of connecting to the world that are decidedly enfleshed, embodied, and earthy and in which relationships aim toward generosity, love, and justice rather than instrumentalism, narcissism, or apocalyptic dread. The language of incarnation has special meaning for Christians, but its emphasis on the embodiment of justice-seeking love gives it broad relevance. No matter how we identify ourselves in relation to religion, we can be powerfully invested in the question of how life-affirming or world-making practices can be enfleshed in today's world. It is true that virtual practices can help create and sustain worlds of healing, but what about actual, in-the-flesh embodiments of world making? In truth, the possibilities for such incarnations are endless. In what follows we lift up a handful of concrete manifestations as illustrations and, more importantly, as invitations to others to create or identify their own examples.

Located at the boundary between the digital and the embodied is today's Maker movement. What began as the transgressive forays of computer hackers into virtual worlds has grown into a wide-ranging cultural phenomenon that celebrates making over consuming and collaboration over competition.[23] Maker Faires and Mini-Maker Faires in diverse cities attract hundreds of thousands of people each year and serve as showcases, laboratories, and meet-up opportunities for countless inventors, designers, builders, tinkerers, and artisans. One maker may use a 3-D printer to create custom frames for eyeglasses while another resurrects the domestic art of canning. The relatively low cost of high-tech machine tools and materials means making goes far beyond the provenance of affluent hobbyists; nevertheless, the sharing of tools and work spaces is a defining feature of the Maker movement. In the thick of global capitalism's digital revolution, this movement manifests a world in which hands-on

workmanship, do-it-yourself ingenuity, small-batch production, and the virtues of collaboration and sharing stand in
sharp contrast to mass-produced consumer culture and the
attendant alienation and injustices it perpetuates. Combin-
ing technological innovation with traditional knowledge and
a genuine regard for craft, Maker culture can be seen as an
incarnational practice of meaning making. The movement
responds to the dystopian dynamics of twenty-first-century
existence with hopeful realism—a kind of stubborn incarna-
tionalism or embodied hope—that staves off cynicism and
despair with handmade beauty and quotidian utility.

Hopeful realism is also apparent on today's college and
university campuses in increased student commitment to
civic or community engagement. No longer satisfied with
learning experiences that are confined to classrooms or that
privilege theory over practice, today's students want learning
to be *real*, to make a difference in the world. They want to
embody the ideas they are learning, to test the validity and
value of concepts and theories through research and action
projects where the stakes are real and the outcomes matter, not only to faculty members, prospective employers, or
a graduate school admissions team but also to off-campus
partners and communities. Where previous generations of
college students were typically motivated to undertake community work by a desire to "serve the less fortunate" or help
the needy, today's students are more likely to see community
members as cocreators of shared work instead of as victims
or as recipients of charity. The widespread shift on college
campuses from community "service" language to community
"engagement" language is an attempt to acknowledge that
instead of a patron-client relationship in which the higher-
education community plays the role of the generous donor of
knowledge and resources that are (or should be) graciously
but passively received by the have-nots, what actually tran-
spires in most cases is a mutual exchange of gifts and graces.[24]
Framed as an experience of partnership instead of patronage,
and based on assumptions of mutuality rather than mastery,
community-engaged work becomes a site for the cultivation

of wonder in the midst of fragility and moral ambiguity and in spite of injustice, oppression, and apocalyptic dread. Such practices are for many young people acts of faith, rooted in religious traditions and yet often exceeding the bounds of any single tradition. Christian, Jewish, Muslim, Hindu, Buddhist, Yoruba, Baha'i—the distinctions are by no means immaterial, and yet even in the midst of considerable differences of belief, religious adherents, searchers, and skeptics find common ground in shared practices for the common good.[25]

Such community-engaged efforts open practitioners' eyes to worlds of experience never before encountered—the daily struggle of low-wage workers for dignity and a living wage; the lack of resources but not of hard work and hope in an inner-city school; the stereotype-smashing wisdom, expertise, and resilience of one's community partners. As we dig into the challenges and possibilities of specific times and places, following the lead whenever possible of those whose well-being is most at stake, we can appreciate the importance of place-based thinking and living. If we look at our own city, neighborhood, or institution with hearts awakened to wonder, what injustices require prophetic protest, what wounds and losses shall we lament, and what life-giving work begs to be done?

Most American cities are places of contradiction. They are prosperous and poor; livable and inhumane; diverse and segregated; well-nourished and craving food. Austin, Texas, the fastest-growing large American city, presents these contradictions vividly. The west side of Interstate 35—home to the University of Texas, high-tech corporate headquarters, and a relatively prosperous Anglo (white) population—houses a veritable foodie heaven. Restaurants that serve cuisine grown, raised, and prepared locally lie near a plethora of supermarkets, farmers' markets, and boutique food stores. This part of town is also home to Whole Foods, a business that began in the 1970s as an alternative hippie market that has now grown into an international marketing colossus. The mother ship in downtown Austin provides a feast for the senses: wandering the aisles, we can dip organic strawberries in a fair-trade chocolate fountain, sample locally grown produce, and buy farm-raised Texas catfish or coho salmon flown from Alaska.

By contrast, the neighborhoods east of Interstate 35 tell a different story. The majority of the city's Latino/as and Blacks live here, and there is no Whole Foods franchise. Among the far fewer places to eat are fast-food chains. Most residents of the east side do not live within walking distance of a full-service grocery store, which prevents securing wholesome food without a car. For many, a convenience store or a greasy burger pose the easiest dining option. According to the US Department of Agriculture, swaths of East Austin are food deserts—places where access to nutritious and affordable food is severely limited. There is much here to protest and lament. In this city of plenty, in this nation of abundance, the foods we eat (and do not eat) reveal the contradictions and injustices of our society. *What* we eat depends on *where* we live. Every American city has its own unique food deserts.

Theology taps unique resources to address these and other socioecological crises. In this instance, it sorts through and reenvisions Christian traditions to better support food justice. Christian traditions, Scriptures, and practices are replete with references to food. Indeed, the first task God gives humanity is to till the garden and keep it.[26] The broad arc of the Christian Bible begins in a garden (Genesis) and ends in a city (Revelation). This movement represents not simply a shift from agrarian to urban contexts. The New Jerusalem of Revelation depicts a garden in the center of the city, a tree of life with abundant fruits for all, where the nations find healing. These images portray no romantic return to Eden but rather bespeak the renewal of the city (created by human hands) and the earth (created by God). In this new city, there are no food deserts, but abundance for all.

Likewise, the Hebrew Scriptures are filled with stipulations about caring for the land, especially the practice of Sabbath. As Ellen Davis writes, "The Scriptures of ancient Israel know where they come from. They reflect the narrow and precariously balanced ecological niche that is the hill country of ancient Judah and Samaria. . . . The Israelite farmers knew that they survived in that steep and semiarid land by the grace of God and their own wise practices."[27] The land is not meant to be worked without end for a maximum yield (a practice that in part contributed to the Dust Bowl of the US prairies in the 1930s) but must experience the rest that sustains the rhythms of creation: "For six years you shall sow your land and gather in its yield; but the seventh year you shall let it rest and lie fallow, so that the poor of your people may eat; and what they leave the wild animals may eat" (Exod. 23:10–11). Here, care for the earth, its creatures, and the well-being of the poor coincide. Rest is essential so that all might live more fully; it is both humane for workers and sound ecological practice. Furthermore, Sabbath is grounded in a God who takes time to rest and delight in creation. Rest is essential to our enjoyment of food, creation, and one another. Without rest, we work ourselves and the land to the bone, depleting the soil so that we must add millions of tons of fertilizer and pesticides to it each year.

The ministry of Jesus often centers on food. Repeatedly, Jesus appears in the Gospels with bread in his hands and wine in his cup. The Gospel writers painstakingly record the meals that Jesus shared: he invites others to share food with him and sometimes even invites himself to dinner (Luke 19:5). Apparently, Jesus' sharing of meals prompted some to accuse him of enjoying food and drink too much (Matt. 11:19). Not surprisingly, the last thing Jesus does with his disciples is share a meal—a meal that Christians remember every time the Eucharist, also known as Communion or the Lord's Supper, is celebrated. In this ritual shared by Christian people from across the globe, practices of eating and drinking become sites of both life-giving connection and of lament. If current American practices and attitudes about food convey economic assumptions about the scarcity of food and the resulting inevitability of food deserts, the Lord's Supper presents strikingly different attitudes about food and the economy. First, at this Table, we meet God not in the raw elements of creation or agriculture but in foodstuffs that are produced by human labor: wheat ground into flour and baked into bread, grapes pressed and fermented into wine. The elements of the Lord's Supper represent the bounty of the earth, which God creates, *and* the countless hours of human labor that go into preparing the feast. In them, God blesses the earth and the work of human hands, offering us Christ in the midst of them. Second, the economic assumption of this Table is not scarcity but abundance. No matter how many are gathered around the Table, there is always room for more. The foods of this Table—the staple, bread, and the drink of celebration, wine—are meant to be shared with all, so that all might be nourished and celebrated. This meal is savored in the company of others; it connects practitioners to God, to earth, and to others both near and far. In it, an ethics of community and of abundance yield an alternative economy in which an increasingly interdependent community joins care for the worker and the earth with care for one another, especially the poor.

Christians throughout history have been called to find life and cultivate it in the midst of deserts. We have already seen how the prophet Ezekiel, when faced with dry bones as a staggering image of death, saw the breath of God bring new life: bone binding to bone; flesh covering sinews. In today's world, the practice of gardening offers one possibility for nourishing life in food deserts. Throughout history, people have gardened. In the midst of a Roman economy that sought to control the production and trade of food, early Christian monasteries tended gardens that represented an alternative economy of food. Benedict stressed the importance of manual labor for all monks, chief of which was agriculture: "When they live by the labor of their hands, as our fathers and the apostles did, then they are really monks."[28] These early monastic communities, almost without exception, established themselves far away from Roman centers of commerce, often in areas that others considered uninhabitable. In such places, the monks created gardens, relying not on corridors of trade but on nursing the land so that it might yield sustainable fruit, turning food deserts into gardens where the bounty of the land was shared. In these communities, the monks relied on the hand of God in creation and the labors of their hands, and they extended hospitality to others. Food, in this economy, was not a medium of exchange but a gift to be shared.

Those who garden today find their connections to soil, rain, and wind more evident, as they droop over struggling tomato plants and drip with perspiration in the summer heat; as hands get dirty tilling soil and feel the worms that fertilize each plant as they burrow and dig deeper. Gardening, in its unique way, represents the cooperation of fruitful labor: the hard work of human hands applied to the soil, water, and sun that God provides. In the food desert of East Austin, Urban Roots offers paid internships for youth to work on a 3.5-acre sustainable farm, which yields approximately thirty thousand pounds of produce per year that go to local food banks and community farmers' markets. Similarly, the Food Project in the metropolitan Boston area creates a community of youth and adults from diverse backgrounds who work together to build a sustainable food system. They annually produce a quarter of a million pounds of pesticide-free produce on seventy acres in Boston, Lynn, Lincoln, and Beverly, Massachusetts. Thousands of pounds are donated to local hunger relief efforts. Both Austin's Urban Roots and Boston's Food Project started small, the vision of a small group of committed people out to change the pernicious cycles of poverty and illness through the simple healing properties of working the soil and growing healthful food. In both programs, the young people learn nutrition and sustainable agricultural practices, and they come to understand the relationships between food, power, and poverty. Meanwhile the farms increase access to wholesome food in poorer neighborhoods of the city.[29] At their best, gardens can represent a microcosm of a locally produced, sustainable harvest, an echo of ancient religious traditions surrounding food and table. Alone, no garden will change the unsustainable and unjust forms of food production in the nation or around the globe. Nonetheless, each attempt at attending to the land, the fruits of the earth, and the labors essential to gathering the harvest bears witness to alternative ways of considering food: our labors are not reduced to marketplace commodities but become occasions for us to take part in a feast where there is always room for more at table, for more opportunities to nurture a garden in the midst of a desert.

Practicing the Body of Christ

Attention to Christian practices of hope and healing make clear that when we say that God so loved the world to become of the world in Jesus, we are saying, *theologically*, that bodies are important. The biblical claim in the creation story of Genesis that human beings are made "in the image of God" (Gen. 1:27), or in Latin, *imago Dei*, is a bodily claim. This means that bodies are not, for example, simply containers of souls; they are modes of wisdom and agency. Black Lives Matter is a courageous and hopeful movement on behalf of real bodies, and those *bodies matter to God.* The Occupy movement was a widespread action based in the belief that material wealth concentrated in the hands of very few is about real bodies suffering in deepening global poverty under the weight of bloated corporate power, and those *bodies matter to God.* So when theology attends to bodies, it is attending to God's own image—not necessarily only as human, but as embodied creatures, and all that have bodies therefore *matter to God.* So bodies are not just containers; they too communicate aspects of God, they embody spirit and possess sacred worth. This suggests that not only is it important to explore the function of race, gender, sexuality, and other markers attributed to bodies, but further exploration into the crucial function of bodily communications in *all* kinds of human encounters is crucial for theology that takes the biblical notion of the image of God seriously.

We can think of the modes of wisdom that reside in bodily practices as bodily skills. Sociologist Pierre Bourdieu uses the idea of *habitus* to describe pre-reflective, or preconscious, bodily knowledge. Not only does *habitus* describe pre-reflective ways of being, *habitus* combines identity with flexibility in a way that he terms "improvisational." Fencing, dancing, and tennis illustrate such bodily knowledge that occurs as "a permanent disposition, embedded in the agents' very bodies in the form of mental dispositions, schemes of perception and thought, . . . which enables each agent to engender all the practices consistent with the logic of challenge and riposte..." Furthermore, such bodily wisdoms entail what Bourdieu calls "regulated improvisation," that is, the ability to do something differently in a new situation.[30] A tennis player, for example, can constantly read and react to every move of her opponent, even before her opponent's play is complete—a "reading" that is not the rapid mental selection of the proper response to fit each of the opponent's responses but "a knowledge and a remembering in the hands and in the body," as sociologist Paul Connerton puts it.[31] She "knows" how to play tennis in always-changing settings. Worship practices in particular communities, to take another example, include the bodily performances and hand or arm waving that will accompany congregational singing and choir performances. There are no prescribed cognitive rules that direct these bodily performances, yet worshipers shaped in these traditions know how to move their bodies even with new hymns and musical performances. And these habituated bodily movements communicate belonging.

Whether cultural or religious, social identities are dependent upon and constructed out of social memory. The most obvious medium of social memory occurs through narratives and symbols. Take Christian identity, for example. A Presbyterian community draws upon basic biblical narratives of Jesus and the God who is present as creator/redeemer/Holy Spirit, and it also depends upon themes from the Protestant Reformation, from John Calvin to modern sources such as the Barmen Declaration or Confession of 1967 to flesh out that biblical story. These normative memories are what Connerton would term *practices of inscription*. Such practices involve the sedimented meanings of a community's tradition—in other words, meanings that can be saved, such as written texts.[32] But equally constitutive of social memory, and thus identity, are *practices of incorporation*, otherwise known as bodily practices. These are the practices that convey their meaning in the performance, like kneeling, standing, bowing heads, or sitting in particular ways. Not understandable simply as the *expression* of the values of the community, wherein the bodies of community members are simply the medium of symbolic meanings, incorporative practices are where "the transmission [is] occuring only during the time that their bodies are present to sustain that particular activity."[33] Thus the savable memory of biblical stories or a sermon is not the only way in which Christian identity is constructed. Performative bodily communications may resonate in some ways with these practices of inscription, but very often they are communicating differently and need much more attention from theologians.[34]

Wonderful examples that have received much attention by church historians and sociologists are found in church traditions of many black communities.[35] In an ethnographic study at Good Samaritan Church in Durham, North Carolina, for example, the feel and sound of the service was not confined to black worship traditions—indeed, the first pastor was a working-class white man. But black call-and-response rhetorics were crucial to every service.[36] Communications over and above the content of Bible reading or the sermon generated the joy, love, and energy of the service. Traveling movements of the minister, excited bursts of noise, banter, and ongoing call-response were typical of this worshiping community. Ritual practices of movement with song, especially the erotic aesthetic of praise songs, and the constant verbal connections with members of the congregation were all obvious producers of pleasurable effects. The back-and-forth was essential to preaching, as assenting noises and nodding heads. A sermon that didn't get "Amen!" and "Preach it!" would not be considered a sermon by the congregation. A loud, clear black male voice typically offered "Hello!" or the basic "Amen" or "Ain't it the truth." While never doing the same thing for all of the worshipers, these practices did produce pleasure in the congregants and a sensibility of God's living presence.[37]

Outsider Wisdom and Healing

Different churches reflect different cultures, and they all exhibit regular and sometimes regulated bodily practices that denote belonging and, eventually, become synonymous with being religious. Think of a church community in which members are expected to enter quietly, music is played in hushed tones, and the sensibility of the worship overall is that God moves in silence or mysterious quiet. Or think of church services that have big bands, swaying music, and expectations that real worship requires rhythm. And there are many other examples, all of which can be tied to culture, and sometimes to race and class. In just about every case the congregation lives into a *habitus*, an unspoken set of expectations and regulations of behavior.

Such habits are so strong that it is usually discordant or unfamiliar bodily practices that bring to light the habits a community has in worship. The study of Good Samaritan United Methodist Church mentioned above provides an example of a church where the participation of some unusual worshipers helped to illuminate the ways that bodily practices (sitting, standing, singing, responding, being quiet) form church communities as much as, or perhaps more than, liturgies or doctrines. We can glimpse through its example that "church" is a form of world making through ritual and regular practices. Church worship habits signify, to its members, what "being Christian" may mean. This suggests that, theologically speaking, there is significance in bodily practices in the formation of the idea of church itself. Theologians call this concern with what church is or should be *ecclesiology*, though very few think about it in terms beyond liturgies and doctrines.

At the time of the ethnographic study, Good Samaritan not only was an interracial church community—a fact that already created attention and tensions in the bodily practices of worship—but the church also invited people from a nearby group home called Wellspring to join them for worship. While most churches in the United States claim to be welcoming of all, it is also the case that very few are *actually* welcoming of people who exhibit distinct physical differences from the majority of the community. This is especially so in the case of people with disabilities, whether due to lack of physical access or the norms for standard worship in most churches. As Nancy Eiesland says, "The body practices of the church are a physical language . . . (which) reveal the hidden 'membership roll,' [of] those whose bodies matter."[38] The following vignette illustrates what we mean:

> When people from Wellspring began to worship regularly at Good Samaritan Church, their behavior was not typical of either the more sedate style of the white Protestant worshipers or the more robust worship of the Black Church tradition. But Pastor Gerald, the black Bahamian minister, was particularly good at welcoming the Wellspring residents. He called each of them by name as they arrived, and they received his back-and-forth banter with them enthusiastically during the official welcome.
>
> When the children's choir sang "He's Got the Whole World in His Hands," their response was immediate. A number of the Wellspring residents came alive. Kay, a large white woman, circled with her arms to the music and gestured to us as if saying, "You there, the whole world, God's got you in his hands!" Terry, who usually sat with her head bowed and eyes closed, rocking backward and forward, seemed to become more alert. She swayed, bobbing her head in ways that seemed in sync with the music. A still younger white man who looked as if he had Down syndrome clapped at the end after moving to the music. Tim, in his wheelchair, grinned during this song and managed to clap.
>
> There was clapping when Pastor Gerald finished and excitement in the air. Then the Praise Team stood up to sing. A black woman sitting next to me handed her baby

girl to her husband and went up to join them. Singing "I Feel the Spirit"—labeled an Act of Praise in the bulletin—seemed to perform in a full-bodied way the joy and pleasure that the community expressed verbally during the sermon. Betty, the first black woman to join the church, led the singing. A back-and-forth between Betty and the rest of the choir was picked up by many of the worshipers. It was like a different language being spoken—a language of movement that was rhythmic and powerful. White worshipers often seem less familiar with this embodied "language"; often they have been taught to be uncomfortable with the dance of worship. But at Good Samaritan it gripped almost everybody. The choir swayed. Sitting a few seats down from me, Betty's husband, Ronnie, mouthed the words and sang along as if it were the most natural thing in the world. Pleasure was palpable in the room.

As a model for a concept of "church," several things become evident. Regimented quiet, hierarchies of who speaks or sings (and when), even patterns of acceptable outbursts, are out the window. When theologians take up the question of what "church" is (what we call "ecclesiology"), Good Samaritan and others like it challenge us to think carefully about what that term means. The members of Good Samaritan are quite clear: this is church.

In the middle of this, Kenny started clapping. An attendant spoke gently to him, asking him to stop, but he kept it up. Then Deborah yelled, "Stop!" and Kenny went silent. Such disruptions had no effect on Pastor Gerald. Without a pause, he offered a pastoral prayer, speaking eloquently of the community's concerns. During the prayer, Kenny started clapping again, and this time he was left alone. At the close of his prayer, Gerald led the congregation in the Lord's Prayer, and it was time for the ritual with the most movement, the sharing of the peace, during which much hugging and noise occurred.

Even more bodily communications are evident in the special service held once a month on Thursday nights, a service specifically for the members of the group home. Gerald welcomed the Wellspring folks in booming, rich tones as they entered for the Thursday night service, again calling each member by name. Some wandered into the sanctuary as if by accident; some walked in haltingly, slowly. Some of the congregants were wheeled in by attendants and parked near the pulpit. Cathy, a white middle-aged woman, strode in with her arms stretched straight out for a hug. About thirty people gathered to worship as the room filled with sounds of delight mixed with other, harder-to-identify noises. The order of service at Thursday night worship was fairly traditional. Opening announcements, call to worship, hymns, sermon, and sharing the peace were basic, just as in most United Methodist churches. At these Thursday night worship services, each element simply underwent a twist to adapt to participants' capacities. Gerald started the announcements by asking, "What's new?" Bill has been to Virginia Beach, or so translated Johnny, the only one who could understand him. "Beach" set off a reaction; the delighted cry "beach!" was heard from several places in the room. Gerald called for a round of applause for Bill. As everyone clapped, Bill's face was split with smiles. New people were introduced and got a hand, too. Gerald intoned a familiar call to worship and the community echoed each line back. Some said it, some said something like it. The sound was chaotic, rich, and more textured than the clear, etched noise of a group speaking sedately in unison.

One of the highlights of the service was always music. Rita, the church pianist, was there to accompany. Regular members Lina and Richard were also there and handed out musical instruments to the participants. The energy level rose visibly with the start of hymn singing. Philip, who had Down syndrome, popped up out of his seat, walked to the front, and took the mike. Ignoring the pastor's attempt to turn him to face the community, Philip sang the entire hymn with his back to us. Some in the group shook tambourines, and a few played cymbals or clacked rhythm sticks together. As we clapped for Philip after the hymn, he raised his arms in a victory salute, then flexed his muscles as he struck a bodybuilder pose. Tim sat thin and curled in his wheelchair; his body trembled a bit. His smile told us that the guttural noises were sounds of joy.

Pastor Gerald read the Scripture lesson about God's giving of the Ten Commandments to Moses (Exod. 20:1–20). Engaging folks as he walked around, Gerald used a large erase board to solicit responses to the story. He sketched a picture of lightning with clouds. "Who is afraid of thunder? Raise your hand." Some raised hands. "Who's afraid of lightning?" More hands. Bob volunteered commentary, and Gerald invited him to come to the front. Bob talked in images of heaven and God and angels. Seeming to speak about his vision, he said, "and lying on your back, the clouds above roll by." Mary, a tiny woman sitting frozen in a wheelchair, began to squeal very loudly. An attendant wheeled her around sideways and began to rub her forehead in a soothing way. Terry sat quietly, head down, and rocked back and forth in her chair.

Gerald next drew stone tablets on the board to represent the commandments. He asked for the community to name the commandments, one by one. Laughing and cajoling and chiding, he got all manner of responses. A couple of participants looked at their Bibles, but it was the job of enumerating the commandments that was taken most seriously. Several hands shot up with fingers raised triumphantly in the air. "First!" then "Two!" "Second," called out several of the men. Getting the "next number" seemed more important than getting the content of the commandment. Gerald wrote them down, and Bob called out, "Love me as you love your neighbor." Gerald chuckled and held him off to get others to speak.

Concluding that love of God is summed up with Jesus' commandment to love our neighbor as ourselves, Gerald asked, "Who is my neighbor?" Diane called out, "ME!" Gerald roared, "Yes, Diane!" and began to name people in the group: "Diane is your neighbor. Bill is your neighbor, Philip and Ralph are your neighbors." He walked around pointing at different people. "And we can do it because God loves us; God helps us. We couldn't do it without God!" A couple of attendants said, "Amen!"

As a great deal of disability literature insists, it is crucial to avoid constructing human subjects primarily through labels that define them simply as broken people.[39] All of us are persons with degrees of disability, and the supposed clear line between the abled and the disabled is a social fiction. The group home population at Good Samaritan Church was distinctive with regard to their inabilities with language, and the lack of various levels of mastery of their own bodies marked them as particularly "different." But these distinctions cannot be allowed to function as a comprehensive, "othering" marker that makes them simply troublemakers.

It is important that the communicative practices of people

without language or with only some language or with different kinds of abilities be understood as communications, and not disruptive behavior. This means that orally delivered content is not sufficient by itself as a communicative form. Nor should it be the principal mode of a community being and becoming church. And yet, most people go to church to hear the sermon or sing the hymns, to sit and stand in unison or to express their faith in familiar ways and feel thereby that they have worshiped God. In large part, what we are saying here is that the medium is part of the message in church (and elsewhere), or at least the medium is as important as the spoken or written message of inclusion. While no church is perfect in its abilities to fully honor the multiple ways that people experience worship or encounter God, what is really distinctive about this story of Good Samaritan and Pastor Gerald was that community's display of a far greater variety of communicative forms than are typical of Sunday morning services elsewhere. The practices of hospitality Pastor Gerald modeled made for a chaotic church environment, but one that enabled every-*body* to be present. What is more, those practices of hospitality didn't seem to harm those members more used to a sedate form for worship. Although they may have at times been the most obvious, loud, or active, the residents of Wellspring were not the only worshipers at Good Samaritan, nor therefore the only recipients of embodied affirmation and prophetic presence.

Bodily practices are thus crucial for theology—the practices of aesthetic movement, dancing, swaying and singing. Bodily knowledge as habituated skills is crucial to the creativity of theology and to theology's attention to the meaning of ritual, worship, and church. Bodily communications found in the nonsymbolic, vibrant and pleasurable practices of the worship services with people from homes like Wellspring are another challenge to the unspoken exclusions practiced by many churches. Rather than disruptions to be disciplined, they are forms of communication that, when honored, turn a church building into the body of Christ.[40] A theological account of the church as a place where the world comes together in praise, lament, prayer, and prophetic witness requires new kinds of recognition like those practiced by the members of Good Samaritan—recognition of the ways that certain practices subtly or not so subtly disable or exclude, and recognition of incorporative practices, practices we have long failed to acknowledge and honor, but practices that are and have always been crucial to our social identity.

The account that theologians give of church, then, needs to do more than discuss purity of doctrine or obedience to liturgical traditions. Theologians also help to identify communities like Good Samaritan that are creating forms of church that embody the values of inclusion and love that we locate at the heart of Jesus' life and teachings. We notice that communities like that *become* the message: "you are welcome here in fact and in practice, whoever and however you are." Saying "welcome" is not enough if by "welcome" what we mean is "come on in and be just like us." Good Samaritan enacted a more real welcome to its neighbors, one that changed the welcoming community and required fundamental shifts in their own expectations of order, decorum, style, and all of the class-based, race-based, and clan-based features of those expectations. Examples like Good Samaritan make clear that "church" is a deeply theological question, and its practices— wherever it is practiced in sanctuaries or far from them—are equally deeply constructive of theology and of the world in which Christians live. Decorous, exclusive church constructs decorous, exclusive theology. At least in practice.

Belief as a Practice of Love

On April 15, 2013, two pressure-cooker bombs were set off just feet from the finish line of the Boston Marathon, resulting in three deaths and dozens of casualties. An international sporting event was suddenly transformed into a war zone, as the National Guard moved in to occupy downtown Boston. *Both* the crowds lining the city streets to cheer the runners along the marathon route *and* the light, swift steps of the runners as they made their way from Hopkinton to Heartbreak

Hill and then to the final turn onto Boylston Street were suspended, as the weight of violence bore down on the city. In the days that followed the event, historic churches became crime scenes, local businesses shut down, and surgeons perched above operating tables to rejoin limbs. The city, many say, was changed that day.

Years after the marathon bombings, there is still the struggle to articulate what this change means. The drive to make meaning can easily slip into a desire to make suffering and violence redemptive. The slogan "Boston Strong" can easily transform into "Boston Strong*er*," meaning that the events need to serve a greater purpose, a greater end. Narrative psychologist Dan McAdams raises concerns about a distinctively American way of interpreting such tragedies. A belief in American goodness and innocence can lead to the demonization of others and to the justification of violent retribution in the aftermath. He warns that interpreting events redemptively often means that strength has to be displayed *at all costs*.[41] These concerns do not downplay the impact of violence or condone the horrible perpetration of such acts. Instead, these concerns ask us to pay attention to how we make meaning in the aftermath.

The muscle memories of such events are difficult to shake. The zombie apocalypse resonates because it bespeaks the dread inside of us, providing images of what we are capable of and what we might become. When Judith Herman mapped the contours of post-traumatic stress disorder in *Trauma and Recovery*, she probably did not imagine that PTSD would become a diagnosis extending far beyond the population she identified. She places the task of restoring trust at the center of trauma healing.[42] Restoring trust is not an abstract mental exercise but rather involves reorienting our senses. As we have seen, the somatic and the spiritual can realign in contemplative practices.

In Christianity, Easter Sunday is one of the most recognized holy days of the year, while its precursor, Holy Saturday, often goes unrecognized. The Apostles' Creed, one of the earliest statements of faith recited by the Christian community, states that following Jesus' crucifixion, death, and burial, "he descended into hell."[43] In the mainstream tradition of interpretation, the descent into hell narrates a voyage in which the Christ, who triumphs over death, demonstrates that victory by preaching to the sinners and unbelievers and by carrying them to heaven in a glorious ascent from the depths of hell to the heights of heaven. Yet other interpretations feature a less triumphant vision in which Christ enters into the experience of hell, not to conquer but to experience it. He enters into the chaos, forsakenness, and alienation of hell. Christ figuratively visits the ghetto. It is a day of mourning and grieving, and it puts a necessary pause on Christian proclamations of new life. The rush to Easter Sunday can often dismiss the realities of death and loss. Several theologians claim the significance of this alternative vision in its less triumphalistic account of Jesus' death and resurrection.[44] Saturday acknowledges the grip of death and the difficulties of envisioning life beyond it. When Christians affirm this pause, they lament—they enter into a vision of solidarity *in* and *with* death.

In a work of theological poetry, *Heart of the World*, Hans Urs von Balthasar identifies Holy Saturday with the chaos and confusion involved in witnessing a world unmaking itself.[45] He narrates simultaneously the descent into hell *and* the disciples' confusion as they linger in the aftermath of the cross. His account blurs the events "above" and "below" ground. In a way, the ground has given way beneath the disciples, and they witness the reaches of death. In the forsakenness of hell, Balthasar tells us, the elements are stirring. A light flickers. A drop of fluid begins to move. Signs of life begin to appear amid the chaos. The images seem rather insignificant—a flicker of light, a drop of water. Yet we are reminded that the images for Spirit, here and in multiple religious traditions, are elemental—air, water, and fire.

During Easter Vigil services on Holy Saturday, the Ezekiel story (which we have mentioned already) of the valley of the dry bones is often read. God instructs Ezekiel to summon the spirit, the *ruach*, from the four winds to bring life where no life can be glimpsed. *Ruach* is translated as breath and wind.

Ezekiel, as directed by God, turns to the four winds and calls out to the *ruach*: "Come from the four winds, O breath, and breathe upon these slain, that they may live" (Ezek. 37:9). As the sinews and skin mix with breath, the prophet guides the movements of a people to new life. In our time, prophetic summons and witness to restoring right relationships, and thereby life, may involve new and multiple modes of communication and connection through digital media, the Maker movement, and community engagement work.

Holy Saturday resonates with posttraumatic realities, in which chaos and confusion reign as the order of the day. The power of Holy Saturday lies in the witness to the ways in which our world unmakes or even destroys us, and yet also in its promise of God's spirit making a new world, a new way *in* and *with* creation. Losing ground, tumbling into chaos under the unbearable weight of violence, the witnesses reconstitute. The elements that *sustain* life arise out of the depths of hell. As the elements rise up, the gardener reaches for the dirt in order to cultivate a garden even amid food deserts.

"I believe in the dirt," Annie said. Each year, a few weeks before graduation, members of the senior class deliver their "This I Believe" statements. Inspired by the 1950s radio program "This I Believe," students are invited to put aside the books and to speak a concise and clear word on their own terms.[46] For some, it is an act of waving good-bye to the professors. For others, it is a call to authenticity. Many students are suspicious of belief language and wrestle with stereotypes about church, dogma, and religious judgment. Rather than provide sophisticated statements about God, they speak more about what they cling to when everything else falls away, a kind of bottom-line trust. This trust, however, is part of the definition of belief, even though it is often overshadowed by a focus on certainty and truth. Annie's trust in the dirt reflects her concerns about the protection of the earth from ecological devastation, early memories of her mother in the garden, and a spiritual pilgrimage she took on the El Camino de Santiago de Compostela.

Annie's statement reflects the posture of contemporary

constructive theology. Trusting in the dirt may be the boldest assertion of belief in uncertain times. Reclaiming the dirt—this basic element, this transformative taproot—inspires the praxis of world making. It enables and sustains both practices of resistance to evil and suffering as well as new religious visions of mutuality, justice, beauty, love, peace, and flourishing emerging from those practices. Constructive theology in this chapter has drawn on resources in Christian and other traditions not only to meaningfully respond to the current realities that threaten creation, but also to reinvent Christianity itself, so that it supports life-giving rather than death-dealing worlds or ways of being and living.

Neither a coping strategy nor an escapist pathology, this trust and its associated practices re-create or remake the world in ways that acknowledge and embrace the limits of human finitude; in other words, these practices cooperate with, instead of replacing, divine agency in an always ongoing and unfinished creation. Trust, then, is not about a flight from a world in peril but a recommitment to it. In this chapter, we bind the question of belief in God to belief in life. Religious belief "calls us to the things of the world"[47] and to practice sustained attention that leads both to lamentation and exuberant, prophetic work. Theology guides us in this sustaining work; it cultivates practices such as wonder that turn us toward rather than away from the vulnerable. Contemplative practices across religious traditions train us to perceive the world anew. In *Spirit and the Obligation of Social Flesh*, Sharon Betcher calls us to a new partnership *with* life, especially when faith in it seems impossible. She identifies this challenge as one of "keeping faith with life."[48] Even when we have lost trust *in* life, we keep faith *with* life by seeking its renewal in unexpected places—in online communities of care, in artisanal cultures, and in urban gardens.

Constructive theologians do not promote these practices—lament, prophetic protest and witness, wonder and contemplation, hope and healing—for the sake of shoring up an apologetic about the truth of Christianity. Instead, these practices are part of the training for the "great-hearted ones" who can maintain trust in and with life. Religious visions and values are often dangerously wielded in times of great anxiety. Incidents of terrorism are often aligned with fundamentalist visions of radical apocalyptic endings and God's purging of creation. As this chapter cautions, glory can often be aligned with these visions. Nonetheless, religious visions of a new creation return us to the heart of constructive theology—to claim these sacred texts, traditions, and practices *otherwise*, for their power to generate compassion and care, and thus to remake a world that teeters on the edge of collapse and coming undone.

God: In Conclusion

The Invitation

The challenge of theology that is truly *awake* to the world—theology that is real—is that it be clear-eyed in its vision of the world in which we live and real in its assessment of the consequences of theological claims in the world. This book has been a journey in which we make explicit just how theology that takes up the challenge of being real, being awake to the world, is done. By asking questions of God, our world, and ourselves from the perspective of those who suffer, this book seeks not only to describe but also to demonstrate what theology looks like when it is *really* concerned about more than fidelity to doctrines or practices, as important as those may be. This is what we mean by theology being real. In these pages a group of constructive theologians have exemplified the hard work of taking seriously the idea that theology matters precisely because its subject is God and it starts from the assumption that the things that God loves matter. So, if we were to place a first marker on this journey, it is the material well-being of God's creation. Our world as it is today, this very moment, is a central theological concern.

This concern for the material well-being of the world that God loves is not just relevant to understanding the shaping of this text. It also reflects our sense of the common ground on which we engage our readers, and what issues and questions they bring to the task of understanding and doing theology. Along the way we have made some assumptions about the readers of this book and have thus tried to speak with them in mind. These assumptions are based on our experiences as scholars, teachers, preachers, friends, and lovers. While certainly informed by research on the religious trends in contemporary America, our reflections come from a deep regard and affection for our students and fellow seekers and lovers of God. Ours has been an attempt to engage the work of theology as an overture of friendship and care, thus our decision to invite others into the process of our work and not to simply pronounce theological conclusions. For a moment, then, let us be transparent about the assumptions about our readers that lie behind this text.

The first assumption we have made is that the readers of constructive theology care. They care about this world. They care about the creatures within it. They care about the Christian faith. They care about God. As we evoke the word "care" we intend more than a passing sympathetic interest. Care implies to us an empathetic response that is substantial enough to pull us into deep engagement, to invest our whole selves into something. It is just this assumption about caring that led to the structure of this book and shaped the ways we identified and addressed the issues on which we have focused. As we suggested in the introduction, there are any number of possible approaches to the task of introducing theology. Our approach is based on the presumption that those who care about racial justice, environmental healing, love in all of its forms, gender equality, building sustainable and just economies, and planetary flourishing seek spiritual pathways and theological resources through which they might join their hearts, minds, and bodies to the living out of a faith that matters.

If our initial assumption about our readers was that they care about God and the things that God loves, our next was that Christian theology has some meaning beyond that of simple academic interest. We do not presume our readers to be churchgoers, but neither do we presume otherwise. Indeed, the collection of theologians who worked together on this project run the spectrum of those who locate their spiritual lives within church communities and those who locate themselves in other sorts of spiritual communities and practices. As we worked together, we talked about readers we hoped to have and imagined them to be seekers for whom the ideas of Scripture, tradition, and Communion, for instance, are not unintelligible even if not part of their common parlance. Our task has been to introduce the core ingredients of constructive theology that give shape to the core passions of constructive theologians (critical and creative knowing, appreciation and appropriation of traditions, and practices of prophetic world making and hope). Even here, though, we have tried to offer enough markers so that those without a religious background (but interest in theology) could orient themselves to our work. Doctrines are not self-explanatory. Even the idea of God needs explanation. Every church community and every generation must run its beliefs through an interpretive lens, making meaning of the ancient words. Throughout this book we have worked to clarify and enlarge the field of inquiry through which traditional theological categories (like God, Church, Salvation and so forth) can be understood, anchoring them in a specific concern for justice and flourishing.

Along the way we have introduced several streams of contemporary constructive theology. Again, we have presumed something here: namely, that the experience of Christian faith is enlivened when shared.[1] For us, this is more than just a presumption about our readers. Those involved with this book teach in colleges, universities, and seminaries. We have seen the ways that new communities and forms of Christian community have emerged and are giving new definition to the Christian faith. For us, then, a significant piece of this work has been the desire to contribute to this new work of the Spirit in ways that are both helpful and generative.

A final presumption underlying all of the work in this text is that our readers are doers. That is to say, our experiences in the classroom, in churches, and on the streets have been that those who are shaping what the Christian faith will be in coming decades are doing so as whole persons in the world, not removed from it. This means that we have emphasized the importance of paying attention to the ways in which concrete individuals and communities enflesh this sort of theological project.

Our hope is that the ideas and stories we have presented in this text enliven each reader's desire to discover a passion for theology that makes a positive difference in the world—to lend a hand, so to speak, in God's love for the world. Starting from this great, messy, magnificently diverse creation of which we are a small part, we understand the universe—all of creation—to be an effect of God's love, indeed synonymous with that love. And, through our interpretations of the Hebrew and Christian Scriptures, we understand God's love to stand resolutely against all that diminishes creation, all that flattens its many differences, all that attempts to eliminate or oppress certain parts for the gain of others.

So we share a deep faith that this sort of theology makes a difference because it does not separate spiritual ills from embodied ones. Spirituality is not a flight from this world but profoundly connected to it. So this sort of theology—again, following Jesus' example, in our case—looks for the connections between peacemaking, justice building, and spiritual wisdom or spiritual aliveness. Christian theology, we maintain, starts where the pain is and works to build a world of healing not only from spiritual pain but from the pain of poverty, injustice, prejudice, and structural oppression *because* "God so loved the world" in all of its messy beauty and struggles. We therefore have confidence in God's ability to use each of our gifts to help make God's love—embodied in creation—ever more materially real. We have done this by way of invitation to join us in constructing theology that, grounded in faith in a God of love, will contribute to our world.

Knowing, Remembering AND Belonging, Acting AND Becoming

This introduction to theology has three large themes: epistemology (knowing), traditions (remembering and belonging), and world making (acting and becoming). We began with the notion of epistemology for several reasons. Perhaps most importantly, we began there because of our sense that insufficient attention is paid to the ways that culture, geographic location, social context, and historical narratives actually shape our experience *and* ideas of God. This contextual shape to what we know (and don't know) is not just true for our relationship with God; it holds as well for our understanding and being in the world. By beginning here, with issues related to how we know what we think we know, we problematize what is perhaps the most contentious issue in theological discussion, right knowing. Who gets to say what about God and what God wants from us can become the basis of schisms, charges of bad faith, and even heresy. The histories of every religion are shaped by arguments about how "right" knowledge of divinity is acquired, transmitted, and interpreted. We realize that even though there are many genuine concerns about understanding God rightly (we too seek to understand God's love rightly), there are power plays in epistemology, making it a very good place to begin.

As constructive theologians we are interested in shifting the conversation about epistemology from squabbles over who knows God best to one that allows for multiple "right" ways of knowing and thinking about God and creation. This means that no one group of Christians (or Muslims, or Jews, or others) has possession of the single right way to know God or to know what God wills. But allowing for multiple right ways still leaves open the question of how to judge, for surely there are some wrong ways. Wouldn't most people agree, for example, that Hitler's demand that the German Christian churches pledge allegiance to the Führer as a recognition of divine favor for the Nazis was a "way" of knowing God that we cannot condone? The question of discernment, we suggest, shifts from institutional authority to effects.

The question becomes, what ways of being in the world are enlivened by particular ways of knowing? By offering this phrasing of the question, we take seriously the role of skepticism in faith as a necessary posture in responsibly claiming the role of interpreter and enflesher of the faith. Being able to look critically at the effects of past claims to knowing God is essential to judging the character of our own claims. What oppressions do we inadvertently overlook or, worse, legitimate? Who is included and who excluded in our understanding? What we learn from careful, faithful, critical thinking about this is never simple, but it helps us to appreciate the power of imagination, both in evoking the Christian faith and in conjuring visions of the world that it might create.

We must take care to remember that we do not make the argument that thinking is superior to experience, only that thinking and experience are inextricably bound. As we noted in our chapter on knowing and not knowing, precisely because the mind/body dichotomy runs deep in our culture and has been used to authorize multiple forms of oppression, it is critically important that we be explicitly attentive to how the relationship between ideas and experience is articulated. As some black theologians have argued, the experience of being black in a racist society changes the *idea* of God when God is portrayed as a white man (as, for example, God is depicted in the famous Sistine Chapel), which in turn can change the experience of God or make it harder to *know* a God of love. The same has certainly been true of many women who have experienced violent abuse at the hands of men, only to be told to worship a male God. This is not to say that human depictions of divinity absolutely rule every human being's individual understanding, but when we are attentive to the relationship between ideas and experience, we may come closer to understanding a God whose existence can—and should—be known in many different ways, according to many different theological approaches. We see such attentiveness to the relationship between ideas and experience as a central part of cultivating the postures that guide the work of constructive theologians. The word "posture" vividly recalls that habits of mind and body shape any and all of our theological reflections. It is precisely what we habitually do, habitually think, and are habitually prone to believe that most shapes our being in and responses to both God and our world.

Habits of mind and of body are not the exclusive domain of individuals. They also shape specific communities. As we demonstrated in our chapter on tradition, it is the habits formed over time through shared stories, repeated practices, and communal experiences that create traditions and bestow identity. Traditions, especially religious traditions, consist of sedimented habits of mind and body that over time lead to the sort of internalized beliefs that give meaning and provide the compass by which people navigate their worlds. In that chapter we suggested that the particularity of traditions are a gift that need not close communities off from others but instead can be sites of celebration (of difference) and of learning (about the multiplicity of ways to God). While we are not naive about the very real ways that religious differences, both within traditions and between them, have provoked so much of the violence and carnage that has scarred human history, we still suggest that the faith held by communities has a greater capacity. Here we have in mind the ways that people of faith in multiple traditions have followed traces of hope in the midst of seeming hopelessness and transformed human history as a result. Dr. Martin Luther King Jr., Mother Teresa, Rabbi Abraham Heschel, the Dalai Lama, and the young leaders of the Black Lives Matter movement are only a few examples of those who bear witness to another way through the ruins. Constructive theology, while focused on the future and believing that we contribute to building it, does not let go of the past in all of its ambiguity. We seek neither to sanitize the terrors of our histories nor to miss the riches of wisdom that run through them—because we are the product of both. In light of this ambiguity, what we know and claim of the traditions that have formed each of us become important sources for theological construction. Textual traditions (the Bible, church creeds, and books of theology), practice traditions (liturgies, feast and festival traditions, individual and communal worship practices), cultural traditions, and important historical events all figure importantly in understanding the diverse pathways on which God calls us and in understanding better the legacies of pain and harm that threaten us still. The challenge for all theologians is to help and not harm, to use our critical and creative energies to support the traditions and habits of the faiths through which God calls even the smallest member of creation by name. It is our calling to think through the Christian traditions in all of their complexity, to contemplate their glories and their warts, to study the texts, to learn and write so that we contribute to others in such a way that they might better embody the life of healing and generosity of spirit to which God surely calls them.

One significant implication of taking seriously the ways in which human beings historically construct systems of knowledge and the ways in which specific traditions shape us collectively is that we must recognize ourselves as creatures with effective agency in the world. Quite literally, this means that together and over time we shape and create worlds. While this might seem like an overstatement, consider the role of culture in the formation of worldviews and the role of worldviews in the physical effects human beings have on the environment and each other. Granting to human beings the capacity to shape and create worlds of meaning that have real material effects in no way impinges on the capacity of God as creator of all that is. Theologians have debated this distinction for millennia, but almost all recognize that human beings have the ability to act, to make decisions that materially affect the world, and that we possess free will in doing so. We are not automatons or puppets on divine strings, and this is both the glory of creation and a source of its pain. There are so many needless wounds in our world, wounds that we can do much to heal if we take more seriously our own power to shape, build, annihilate, or heal that which God's love has created. Reticence to take responsibility for our capacity to shape and create the worlds in which we live has led to the type of irresponsibility that visits devastation on our environment and threatens the very basis of our existence as a species, not to mention the existence of other species.

We are not only capable of destruction in large or small doses. We are also capable of creation, able to respond to God's invitation to us to add our little, local loves to God's love (remember, we understand "creation" to be synonymous with God's love). Constructive theology therefore attends both to prophetic practices of criticism and to lament in order to bring more clearly into view the real lived consequences of our world-shaping histories, but it also attends to practices of healing, however local and idiosyncratic. Maker cultures that are springing up everywhere give hope for practices of well-being in which anyone can participate; contemplative rituals focus on beauty, breathing, humility, and peace as forms of prayer and forms of embodying love in ways that bring more beauty, more breath, more humility, and more peace literally into the world. Local practices of real welcome to strangeness—funny, poignant, chaotic, new— bear witness to the resilience of hope and the capacity we have to remake and reshape worlds of life out of habits of death.

So the worlds we create are intimately connected to the stories and rituals by and through which communities create and maintain their particular identities. This means that traditions and world-making practices are inextricably bound together because what we have identified as examples of world-making practice (prophetic witness, lament, community building, healing, contemplation, and welcome) are each examples of specific theological traditions becoming embodied in the world and so making the world anew. A healthy relationship between the conserving energies of tradition and the creative energies of world making enables and creates imaginative spaces for the renewal and transmission of the stories and practices around which communities gather and remember themselves. These are the theologically rich ways of establishing communal identities of belonging and becoming that not only remember inherited traditions but also are attentive to the memories of others and so enable new knowing, better faith, and more authentic celebrations of difference.

It is possible now to see how clearly the themes of knowing (epistemology), remembering and belonging (traditions), and practices of world making are each prior to the others and yet also derived from the others. What counts as knowledge about the world and about God shapes both traditions and practices, and in turn it is shaped by them. The same dynamic relation is true of each theme. This reflexive dynamism makes the work of theology a present-tense endeavor that at the same time understands and appreciates the ways that history creates and precludes possibilities for the work. In order for this work to be accomplished responsibly we must take a full measure of the world in which we find ourselves, some understanding of how we got here, and exercise imagination about possibilities for a future in which all thrive.

Constructing a Concept of God

Put simply, a doctrine of God is the condensation of what a community thinks, says, and believes it knows about God. So, then, the articulation of a doctrine of God is at once a statement of what a community believes God to be and who they are in relation to that belief. God's omnipotence, for example, not only says something about what a community may mean by the word "God," but it also reveals something of the relationship that they seek with God, as a people who feel powerless, say, or as a people who can only imagine valuing a certain kind of power as worthy of worship. Usually the images people have used for God are human (though not always, as the Hebrew Bible in particular reveals), and this reveals something of the theological imagination of a community, or its limitation. In any case, it can be difficult to remember, as the great theologian Paul Tillich said, that "If a segment of reality is used as a symbol for God, the realm of reality from which it is taken is, so to speak, elevated into the realm of the holy. . . . If God is called the 'king,' something is said not only about God but also about the holy character of kinghood."[2] We have to remember the many ways that words become flesh.[3]

Statements about God—when "God" refers to the creator of all that is—generally reflect not only a sense, or picture, of "all that is" but also deep yearnings for what the world might be and who we might be in it. This is not to say that doctrines of God are only the projections of human hopes and desire, as if God has nothing to do with the matter. It is of course possible to hold to the belief that there is no God at all behind the experiences of millions of people over millennia and to reduce their beliefs and experiences to delusion. But it is impossible to prove that belief (which is a kind of faith as well) and unnecessary to do so. No, for those who are willing to be open to the possibility of God and to the richness of Christian theology, we simply point out that from beginning to end speech *about* God is not the same thing as God. Speech about God is the speech of flesh-and-blood human beings and so subject to every enthusiasm or error in judgment to which human beings are wonderfully prone. Furthermore, because whatever it is that a community says about God is said with language and ideas framed by language and culture, this speech will then have a specificity that locates it in time, culture, and place. And if we take seriously our own example of the Good Samaritan church community in Durham that understands the nonverbal multiplicity of ways that theology is enacted in practices and habits of worship, the same holds true. Whatever a community bodily enacts in its practices of worship of God reveal what it thinks and teaches about God. This is another way of saying that doctrines of God, whether they admit it or not, are creatures of the here and now. Consequently, even commonplace assertions like "God is the creator of all" are necessarily framed by what a community understands the world to be, which significantly includes *how* the world exists for them in that time and place. Lived realities and experiences certainly affect how individuals and communities come to believe that God relates to them, and how God relates to them (and if God relates to them).

To illustrate what this can mean, let's turn to the first words

of the Christian Bible and of the Jewish Torah: "In the beginning God created the heavens and the earth" (Gen. 1:1). This
is a theological claim that, while many Christians and Jews
hold it to be true, cannot be demonstrated through any sort
of cosmic mechanics that we understand; the limits of our
capacities as human beings preclude that possibility. Thus,
claims like this about God are rooted in something other than
scientific or mechanistic descriptions. The importance of this
point is that theological accounts of how God works within
creation are likewise not reducible to scientific or mechanistic explanations alone. Rather, the truth of the poetry in Genesis 1 is rooted in the ground from which we judge the truths
of Scripture and of traditions: namely, the vastly complex category of human experience. This experience, given voice in
the witness of Scripture and carried forward by those who
sought God and loved their neighbors throughout human
history, has been that God's presence is most vividly experienced in times of trouble and most authentically experienced
in times of flourishing. From this witness, theologians can
then draw implications about God's deep compassion in the
world that shape our experience and readings of both Scripture and tradition.

By locating God's presence and activity in the complexity
of lived experience, we must take up the question of what we
know of that experience: whether we have listened to enough
and different voices, attended to the verbal as well as the
silenced and nonverbal communications to better understand
the rich media through which God reaches out to us. This
epistemologically humble approach to the doctrine of God
gives primacy to the category of relationality because of our
belief that humanity speaks most truthfully about the experience of God from the depths of our experience of life.

If the primary category for speaking about God is relationality, then the goal of constructive theological discourse
is a deeply interrelated vision of planetary flourishing as
a form of worship of God. Most theological streams have
their touchstone in Scripture, and one verse that could well
nourish this approach to theology is in the Gospel of John,

where Jesus says: "I came that they may have life, and have it abundantly."[4] Life in its abundance becomes a guiding image for constructing a concept of God that attends to what we know about the world that is ending and the worlds that are emerging all around us, that is faithful to our traditions without being enslaved by them, and that gives guidance to our practices of prophetic protest against the forces that diminish life, of lament for those kept from flourishing, of community building and healing that grow networks of support and celebration, and of contemplation of life in its simple, even transient fullness and grace. This does not mean that we ignore those stories in the Bible or parts of the tradition in which death is discussed or even idealized. What it does mean is that Christian theology that is both awake to this moment and alive with hope seeks out traces in its written and practiced traditions of God as the One who not only brings life into being but is the One who treasures life and holds each one precious and near. With a sense of *this* God, there is no excusing abuse of power, corporate or private avarice, or other diminishments of life for the benefit of a few. Changing a concept of God from a distant, judgmental ruler to a relational lover of creation may not cure the world's powermongers or end the vicious cycles of racism and poverty that so diminish us all. But we can begin to see how concepts of God work at the deepest levels of communal imagination, subtly shaping values and hemming horizons of possibility. Is it any wonder that people choose simply to leave their faith communities when all they can see in them are embodied practices of cruel judgment or banal irrelevance? Constructive theology takes the position that there is so much more capacity in God than we know, remember, or imagine. There is great work to do here.

Constructing Theology

The spirit of the Lord GOD is upon me,
  because the LORD has anointed me;

he has sent me to bring good news to the oppressed,
    to bind up the brokenhearted,
to proclaim liberty to the captives,
    and release to the prisoners.

                                      (Isaiah 61:1)

We began this book by saying that the idea of God is central to the Christian faith both in its self-understanding and in its apprehension of the world. Here we return to that idea equipped with a fuller sense of what this means in the real world, where pressing problems challenge us from every angle. One task for the faithful in each generation is that they give account of how their belief in God guides them toward more critical and creative ways of knowing, into deeper appreciation of the many traditions that shape faithful living, and toward practices that bring flourishing to God's creation. There is ambiguity in this task because no one account can cover the life of all creation even in a single generation. Lives unfold differently in differing locations shaped by different histories. But we have argued that the ambiguity such diversity creates is not a problem to be solved. Rather, it is an opportunity for theologians to attend to the specificity of communities, to support the ways that they give shape to faith in their own settings, and to assist them in more fully embodying the love that God expresses in the fulsome diversity of creation.

We also said in the introduction to this book that Christian theology is a blend of human and divine, of imagination and revelation. All theology, we said, is constructed out of the best efforts of human beings to understand the ineffable reality and experience of divinity in the world. And theology always must be treated with a mixture of credulity and criticism. Like human hearts, theology is always undergoing improvement so long as it remains open. This means, we can say now in conclusion, that theology is a work of individuals and communities, and it is both real and awake when it attends to real lives and lived consequences. Further, theology requires the explicit engagement of whole persons in the fullness of creation that God so loves. Constructive theology can contribute

to the flourishing of creation by naming, lamenting, and confronting those powers and ways of being that yield suffering
and death. But theology awake to the world does not stop
there. It seeks and finds tender shoots of new life struggling
to emerge in even the deepest corners of diminished and
hunted life. This theology names, celebrates, and encourages each local movement of protest on behalf of the living,
each dance step of healing, each bird in flight that blesses the
world anew with its holy, graceful spirit. This, we suggest by
way of closing a book only to open a challenge, is doing theology in a way that matters.

Notes

Introduction

1. Luke 10:29–37.
2. *The Blacklist*, season 3, episode 4, "The Djinn (No. 43)," directed by Omar Madha, screenplay by Daniel Cerone, NBC, October 22, 2015.
3. John 8:32.
4. Isa. 61:1 and Luke 4:18.
5. Richard Viladesau, *The Beauty of the Cross: The Passion of Christ in Theology and the Arts from the Catacombs to the Eve of the Renaissance* (Oxford: Oxford University Press, 2006), 156–57.
6. Anselm, *Proslogion: With the Replies of Gaunilo and Anselm*, trans. Thomas Williams (Indianapolis: Hackett Publishing, 2001).
7. James H. Cone, *God of the Oppressed*, rev. ed. (Maryknoll, NY: Orbis Books, 1997).

What Do We Know and How?: Context and Questions

1. All that remains of Heraclitus' writings are fragments, quoted in other ancient philosophers. Plato quoted him several times in his dialogue *Cratylus*. For example, "all things are in motion and nothing at rest" *Cratylus* 402a (Charleston, SC: Bibliobazaar, 2007), 97.
2. Alfred Lord Tennyson, "In Memoriam A.H.H." in *Poems of Tennyson with an Introduction by T. S. Eliot* (London: Thomas Nelson & Sons LTD, 1935), LV, 372.
3. John 16:13.
4. Augustine, *Tractates on the Gospel of John*, 29.6.
5. Anselm, *Proslogion*, 1.

6. John Calvin, *Institutes of the Christian Religion,* ed. John T. McNeill (Louisville, KY: Westminster John Knox Press, 1960), I.13.1.

7. See Ann Weems, *Psalms of Lament* (Louisville, KY: Westminster John Knox Press, 1995), Walter Brueggemann, *Psalmist's Cry: Scripts for Embracing Lament* (The House Studio: 2010), and Cynthia L. Rigby, "Providence and Play," *Insights* I.21, vol. 2, 10–18.

8. According to a 2012 report from the Public Religion Research Institute, one-third of Americans under the age of thirty are unaffiliated with a formal religious group. This is an all-time low in American history. While only 10 percent of people who are fifty and older say religion is unimportant in their lives, 20 percent of persons aged eighteen to twenty-nine say religion makes no difference to them at all (http://publicreligion.org/site/wp-content/uploads/2012/10/AVS-2012-Pre-election-Report-for-Web.pdf). For a full development of the "spiritual but not religious" phenomenon, see *Belief Without Borders* by Linda Mercadante (New York: Oxford University Press, 2014).

9. Eric Weiner, "Americans: Undecided about God?," opinion column, *New York Times*, December 10, 2011.

10. "In 'Man Seeks God,' Author Eric Weiner Hunts for Divine Meaning," PBS Newshour, December 26, 2011, www.pbs.org/newshour/bb/religion-july-dec11-manseeksgod_12-26/.

11. "Of Myth and Men: A Conversation between Bill Moyers and George Lucas," *Time,* April 26, 1999, 92.

12. From John Calvin's definition of faith, in *Institutes of the Christian Religion* III.2.7, ed. John T. McNeill, trans. Ford Lewis Battles (Philadelphia: Westminster Press, 1960).

13. Audio of the Q&A with Christian Wiman at Christ Episcopal Church in Charlottesville, VA, on May 17, 2013, can be found at http://www.christchurchcville.org/sermons-series/an-evening-with-christian-wiman-q-a/.

14. Lehmann taught theological ethics at Princeton, Union, and Harvard throughout the mid-twentieth century. He was great-uncle to one of the contributors to this volume (Laurel Schneider), and she recalls his younger cousin Hilda relating his fondness for repeating this statement of belief and non-belief. Apparently he also said it to his students. Fleming Rutledge quotes it in "A Tribute to Paul Louis Lehmann" in *The Princeton Seminary Bulletin*, 15, no. 2 (1994): 169.

15. Luke 1:46–55.

16. Marguerite Shuster, *The Fall and Sin: What We Have Become as Sinners* (Grand Rapids: Eerdmans, 285).

17. For some examples of the "Prosperity Gospel" movement, see Joel Osteen, *Your Best Life Now: Seven Steps to Living at Your Full Potential* (New York: Warner Books, 2004), and Creflo Dollar, *You're Supposed to Make Money, Live Comfortably, and Build an*

Inheritance for Future Generations (New York: Faith Words, 2014). Few preachers of prosperity ever achieve the net worth of Osteen and Dollar (estimated at $27 million and $40 million respectively in 2016), and even fewer of their congregants ever get the opportunity to make it into the upper income percentiles.

18. John Wesley, *The Works of the Rev. John Wesley*, ed. Thomas Jackson, 3rd ed. (London: Wesleyan Methodist Book Room, 1872; repr., Peabody, MA: Hendrickson, 1986), 3:178.

19. The German philosopher Ludwig Feuerbach, for instance, asserted in 1841 that all religion is a projection of the human mind. He did not therefore think religion a bad thing, but rather thought it a kind of morality system that could be manipulated at will to improve human life. God is a projection of human imagination and religion a projection of the dominant values of the day. See Ludwig Feuerbach, *The Essence of Christianity* (Amherst, NY: Prometheus Books, 1989).

20. John Wesley, "The General Spread of the Gospel," in *The Bicentennial Edition of the Works of John Wesley*, ed. Albert C. Outler (Nashville: Abingdon, 1987), 2:494; the biblical references are to Heb. 8:11 and Rom. 2:29.

21. Joerg Rieger, *Grace under Pressure: Negotiating the Heart of the Methodist Traditions* (Nashville: United Methodist General Board of Higher Education and Ministry, 2011).

22. René Descartes, *Discourse on Method and Related Writings*, trans. Desmond M. Clarke (New York: Penguin, 1999).

23. Ibid., 24.

24. Ibid., 25.

25. Ibid., 9–10, 13, 17.

26. Ibid., 25.

27. Howard Gardner, *Frames of Mind: The Theory of Multiple Intelligences* (New York: Basic Books, 1983).

28. Damasio's argument is referred to as the somatic marker hypothesis. Antonio Damasio, *Descartes' Error: Emotion, Reason and the Brain* (New York: Putnam Publishing, 1994).

29. Two articles that summarize some of this emerging field are Margaret Wilson, "Six Views of Embodied Cognition," *Psychonomic Bulletin and Review* 9, no. 4 (2002): 625–36 and Michael L. Anderson, "Embodied Cognition: A Field Guide," *Artificial Intelligence* 149 (2003): 91–130.

30. Diana Taylor, *The Archive and the Repertoire: Performing Cultural Memory in the Americas* (Durham, NC: Duke University Press, 2003), 19–20.

31. Paul Connerton, *How Societies Remember* (New York: Cambridge, 1989), 39–40.

32. Ibid., 88.

33. For an interesting, if limited, recent take on this, see Jason Stanley and John W. Krakauer, "Is the 'Dumb Jock' Really a Nerd?," *New York Times*, October 27, 2013.
34. Taylor, *Archive and Repertoire*, 17.
35. Ibid., 17–18.
36. Dwight Conquergood, "Performance Studies: Interventions and Radical Research," in *The Performance Studies Reader*, 2nd ed., ed. Henry Bial (New York: Routledge, 2004), 371. See also the work of postcolonial theorist Gayatri Chakravorty Spivak, "Can the Subaltern Speak?," in *Marxism and the Interpretation of Culture*, ed. Cary Nelson and Lawrence Grossberg (Urbana: University of Illinois Press, 1988).
37. Conquergood, "Performance Studies," 376.
38. John Locke, *The Reasonableness of Christianity*, ed. I. T. Ramsey (Stanford, CA: Stanford University Press, 1958), 31–32.
39. Pseudo-Dionysius, *The Mystical Theology*, http://www.esoteric.msu .edu/VolumeII/MysticalTheology.html. Accessed May 17, 2016. Other apophatic figures include Meister Eckhart, Pseudo-Dionysius, and St. John of the Cross.
40. Albert Schweitzer, *The Quest for the Historical Jesus: A Critical Study of Its Progress from Reimarus to Wrede* (New York: Macmillan, 1964; first English edition, 1910).
41. See the Web site of Organization United for Respect at Walmart at ForRespect.org.
42. Karl Rahner, *Foundations of Christian Faith* (New York: The Seabury Press, 1978), 22.

Tradition in Action

1. For more on this notion of repertoire, see Robert Ford Campany, "On the Very Idea of Religions (In the Modern West and China)." History of Religions, 5/2003, ISSN: 0018-2710, vol. 42, no. 4, p. 316–18.
2. Catechism of the Catholic Church, chap. 2, art. 3, para. 85; citing previous church document *Dei verbum*.
3. Max Weber, *The Protestant Ethic and the Spirit of Capitalism,* trans. Talcott Parsons (New York: Scribner, 1958).
4. The Latin *traditio* finds an echo in the Greek *paradidomi*. This echo offers more grist for the mill because forms of *paradidomi* are found in the New Testament when Paul asserts that he has taught what was "handed over" to him as well as when the stories of Judas's betrayal speak of him "handing over" Jesus to the authorities.
5. Joseph Barndt, *Becoming an Anti-Racist Church: Journeying toward Wholeness* (Minneapolis: Fortress Press, 2011), 28–29.
6. See Temba L. J. Mafico, "Just, Justice" *The Anchor Bible Dictionary*, vol. 3, H–J, David Noel Freedman, ed. (New York: Doubleday,

1992), 1127–29. Cf. James L. Mays, "Justice: Perspectives from the Prophetic Tradition" in *Prophecy in Israel,* ed. David L. Petersen (Philadelphia: Fortress Press, 1987), 144–58.

7. Augustine, *City of God,* XIX.13.

8. Matt. 25:31–45.

9. John Hick, *A Christian Theology of Religions: The Rainbow of Faiths* (Louisville, KY: Westminster John Knox, 1995), 77–78.

10. In *Acts of Faith,* Eboo Patel chronicles the rise of the Interfaith Youth Core. Inspired partly by his Muslim grandmother's service to shelter abused women and partly by his own work with The Catholic Worker as well as interfaith programs, Patel founded the IFYC not to promote religious conversion, coexistence, or consensus but to embrace religious pluralism through interfaith service for the common good. Using IFYC's method, religiously diverse young people discuss shared values, engage in joint social action based on those values, and participate in interreligious dialogue—all to enhance their own religious identity and mutual understanding. Eboo Patel, *Acts of Faith: The Story of an American Muslim, the Struggle for the Soul of a Generation* (Boston: Beacon Press, 2007), xv, 72–74, 164–72, 183–88.

11. For an introduction to faith-rooted organizing, see Alexia Salvatierra and Peter Goodwin Heltzel, *Faith-Rooted Organizing* (Downers Grove, IL: InterVarsity Press, 2013).

12. John Augustine Ryan, *A Living Wage: Its Ethical and Economic Aspects* (New York: Macmillan Co., 1906).

13. For a Catholic feminist response to the issues of women's ordination, see Laura M. Taylor, "Redeeming Christ: Imitation or (Re)citation?," in *Frontiers in Catholic Feminist Theology: Shoulder to Shoulder,* ed. Susan Abraham and Elena Procario-Foley (Minneapolis: Fortress Press, 2009), 118–40.

14. Franjo Cardinal Seper, Prefect, Congregation for the Doctrine of the Faith, *Inter Insignores,* §5, October 15, 1976. Available at www .vatican.va.

15. Ibid.

16. Simone Campbell, "Paul Ryan's Budget Undermines the Best of America," *National Catholic Reporter,* March 25, 2013.

17. Elizabeth Stuart, "Sacramental Flesh," in *Queer Theology: Rethinking the Western Body,* ed. Gerard Loughlin (Malden, MA: Blackwell Publishing, 2007), 68.

18. Martin Luther King Jr., "The World House," in *Where Do We Go from Here? Chaos or Community* (Boston: Beacon Press, 1968), 168.

19. Ulrich Beck, *Cosmopolitan Vision,* trans. Ciaran Cronin (Cambridge, UK and Malden, MA: Polity Press, 2006), 23–24.

Ways of World Making: Practices of Prophecy and Lament

1. Francis, *Laudato Si'* [Encyclical Letter on Care for Our Common Home], sec. 14, accessed May 9, 2016, http://w2.vatican.va/content /francesco/en/encyclicals/documents/papa-francesco_20150524 _enciclica-laudato-si.html.
2. This story is found in the Hebrew Scriptures, Ezek. 37:1–14.
3. "A Zombie Scare with a Zombie Chaser," *New York Times*, June 22, 2013, http://www.nytimes.com/2013/06/23/opinion/sunday/dowd -a-zombie-scare-with-a-zombie-chaser.html.
4. This does not operate just at the level of cognition but at a somatic level. Anxiety works at an affective level. Bessel van der Kolk, *The Body Keeps the Score: Brain, Mind, and Body in the Healing of Trauma* (New York: Viking, 2014).
5. The Institute for Intercultural Studies, Frequently Asked Questions 1–2, http://www.interculturalstudies.org/faq.html, accessed May 9, 2016. The trademark for this quote is held by Sevanne Kassarjian, New York, and is used by permission.
6. Roger S. Gottlieb, *Joining Hands: Politics and Religion Together for Social Change* (Boulder, CO: Westview Press, 2002), 3–23, esp. 4–6, 9, 19–21.
7. Ibid., 20. For example, see Laurie Cassidy and Maureen H. O'Connell, eds., *She Who Imagines: Feminist Theological Aesthetics* (Collegeville, MN: Liturgical Press, 2012).
8. Barbara A. Holmes, "'We'll Make Us a World': A Post-Obama Politics of Embodied Creativity," in *Ain't I a Womanist, Too? Third Wave Womanist Religious Thought*, ed. Monica A. Coleman (Minneapolis: Fortress Press, 2013), 188, 191, and 189.
9. Ibid., 195, 196.
10. Suzanne Collins, *The Hunger Games*, *Catching Fire*, and *Mocking Jay* (New York: Scholastic Books, 2014); Veronica Roth, *Divergent*, *Insurgent*, *Allegiant*, and *Four* (New York: HarperCollins, 2014); and Cormac McCarthy, *The Road* (New York: Vintage Books, 2006).
11. Craig Dykstra and Dorothy Bass, "A Theological Understanding of Christian Practices," in *Practicing Theology: Beliefs and Practices in Christian Life*, ed. Miroslav Volf and Dorothy C. Bass (Grand Rapids: Eerdmans, 2002), 18; see also 21 and 22–29.
12. David H. Jensen, series ed., *Compass: Christian Explorations of Daily Living* (Minneapolis: Fortress Press, 2010–13).
13. Dykstra and Bass, "Theological Understanding of Christian Practices," 6.
14. Ibid., 21; see also 29.
15. The spelling of Dorothee Sölle's name has been altered for English translations and US publications to Soelle. Rosemary Radford Ruether, "The Feminist Liberation Theology of Dorothee Soelle,"

and Beverly Wildung Harrison, "Dorothee Soelle as Pioneering Post-modernist," in *The Theology of Dorothee Soelle*, ed. Sarah K. Pinnock (Harrisburg, PA: Trinity Press International, 2003).

16. Ada María Isasi-Díaz, *La Lucha Continues:* Mujerista *Theology* (Maryknoll, NY: Orbis Books, 2004), 19, 50–51, 177–79; see also Isasi-Díaz, *En La Lucha/In the Struggle: A Hispanic Women's Liberation Theology* (Minneapolis: Fortress Press, 1994), 176–87.

17. Isasi-Díaz, *En La Lucha*, 187.

18. Ibid., 52–54, 181, 183.

19. Ibid., 184.

20. Plato, *Theaetetus*, trans. B. Jowett (Rockville, MD: Serenity Publications, 2009), 104.

21. Karl Barth, *Evangelical Theology: An Introduction* (Grand Rapids: Eerdmans, 1963), 63.

22. Ibid., 64.

23. Ibid., 65.

24. Irenaeus, *Against Heresies,* 4.20.7. There is some uncertainty whether the phrase "fully alive" is the best translation; *Ante-Nicene Fathers* says simply "living."

25. L. Boff and C. Boff, *Liberation Theology: From Dialogue to Confrontation* (San Francisco: Harper & Row, 1986), 25.

26. Elizabeth A. Johnson, *She Who Is: The Mystery of God in Feminist Theological Discourse* (New York: Crossroads, 1992).

27. Elizabeth A. Johnson writes, "If the earth is indeed creation, a sacrament of the glory of God with its own intrinsic value, then for Christians ongoing destruction of earth bears the marks of deep sinfulness." Johnson, "God's Beloved Creation," *America: The National Catholic Review* (April 16, 2001): 11.

28. Enrique Dussel, *A History of the Church in Latin America* (Grand Rapids: Eerdmans, 1981), 307.

29. Walter Brueggemann, *The Prophetic Imagination*, 2nd ed. (Minneapolis: Fortress Press, 2001), 1–19.

30. Helene Slessarev-Jamir, *Prophetic Activism: Progressive Religious Justice Movements in Contemporary America* (New York: New York University Press, 2011), 1–20.

31. Ibid., 4.

32. Ibid., 58–64.

33. Gottlieb, *Joining Hands*, 18–19.

34. Mark Lewis Taylor, *The Executed God: The Way of the Cross in Lockdown America* (Minneapolis: Fortress Press, 2001), 117.

35. Ibid. For more on the theological basis of this theatrics in Christology, see esp. 70–78, 90–118, 127–33.

36. Mark Lewis Taylor, *The Theological and the Political: On the Weight of the World* (Minneapolis: Fortress Press, 2011), 114, 136.

37. Ibid., 12–14, 114; see also chap. 3.
38. Abraham J. Heschel, *The Prophets: An Introduction* (New York: Harper Colophon Books, 1962), 5, 7, 10, 22.
39. Brueggemann, *The Prophetic Imagination*, 40.
40. Sidney Mead, *The Lively Experiment: The Shaping of Christianity in America* (New York: Harper & Row, 1963), 4.
41. Charles Long, *Significations: Signs, Symbols, and Images in the Interpretation of Religion* (Philadelphia: Fortress Press, 1986), 145; David Noble, *Historians Against History* (Minneapolis: University of Minnesota Press, 1965), 176.
42. Exod. 19:9, 11, 16, 19; Pss. 18; 29; 68:4, 7–8; 77:17–18; 104; etc. Yahweh is depicted throughout much of the biblical text as a storm deity, speaking in thunder, pouring out blessing as rain, flooding the land, much like the Phoenician god Baal.
43. When creatures domesticated and enslaved by humans break out and return to the wild, they are said to go feral, to return to their original freedom. In Spanish, the term for such a liberated creature is *cimarron*, which in the Americas is Anglified and used in relationship to escaped slaves, known as "Maroons." Ancient Israel was a "maroon movement" in exiting Egypt, going out into the Sinai wildlands to relearn freedom.
44. "Original gangster"; in hip-hop terms, someone who is not merely a "studio" version, pantomiming the violence artistically, but actually has killed and likely has a record and a warrant outstanding. For instance, according to Michael Eric Dyson, Big Syke, mentor of Tupac Shakur in thug hermeneutics, schooled his protégé to the fact that Moses "was a killa." Michael Eric Dyson, *Holler If You Hear Me: Searching for Tupac Shakur* (New York: Basic Civitas Books, 2001), 212.
45. Brueggemann, *The Prophetic Imagination*, 23–25.
46. Highest mountain in the Zagros range of Iran, just east of what would have been Babylon.
47. Gen. 1:1–2:3 is a narrative composed while Israel was in exile in Babylon that addresses the Baylonian genesis myth, the Enuma Elish (EE), as its immediate object of critique. The EE narrates the god Marduk killing the goddess Tiamat and then dividing her body into upper waters (clouds, rain, etc.) and lower waters (springs, seas, rivers, etc.), which the Hebrew Genesis adapts and alters in its own version of separating the waters of heaven from the waters of earth in Gen. 1:1–10. For a summary commentary on the EE, see Alexander Heidel, *The Babylonian Genesis* (Chicago: University of Chicago Press, 1967), 3–10.
48. The Hebrew word translated "hovering" refers to what a mother eagle does over her nestlings when it is time for them to take the

momentous step out of safety to launch into space; she literally beats them to the nest's edge with her wings.

49. Evan Eisenberg, *The Ecology of Eden: An Inquiry into the Dream of Paradise and a New Vision of Our Role in Nature* (New York: Vintage Books, 1999), 4–7.

50. Technically weeds, whose expansionist bent depends upon disturbances or breaks in the local ecosystem—like plowed furrows or cleared trees.

51. Larry L. Rasmussen, *Earth Community, Earth Ethics* (Maryknoll, New York: Orbis Books, 1996), 40–43.

52. The Natufians were an Epipaleolithic hunter-gatherer culture, dwelling in the Levant from 12,500 to 9500 BCE, who became sedentary, began to harvest wild grains, and developed a symbiotic relationship with almond, olive, lemon, and oak trees; see Eisenberg, *Ecology of Eden*, 7.

53. Isa. 40:6–7.

54. Jews were not the only victims of the Holocaust. "Many other groups were targets of persecution and even murder under the Nazis' ideology, including Germans with mental and physical disabilities, homosexuals, Jehovah's Witnesses, Roma ('Gypsies'), Poles, and Soviet prisoners of war. Millions perished in this state-sponsored tyranny." The United States Holocaust Memorial Museum, "Nazi Persecution of Homosexuals: 1933–1945," accessed at https://www.ushmm.org/exhibition/persecution-of-homosexuals/.

55. Jeffrey Alexander, "On the Social Construction of Moral Universals: The 'Holocaust' from War Crime to Trauma Drama," *European Journal of Social Theory* 5, no. 5 (2002): 44.

56. Ulrich Beck, *Power in the Global Age* (Malden, MA: Polity Press, 2005), 104.

57. Dermot Moran, *Introduction to Phenomenology* (New York: Routledge, 2000), 237.

58. Mark Chmiel, "The Holocaust Museum: Reasons of Memory or Reasons of State," *Ecumenist* 2/3 (July–September 1995): 46.

59. Jürgen Moltmann, contribution to the panel discussion "Hope—After Auschwitz and Hiroshima?" in *The Future of Hope*, edited by Walter Capps (Philadelphia: Fortress Press, 1970), 96.

Ways of World Making: Practices of Contemplation, Connection, and Church

1. Isaac of Nineveh, *On Ascetical Life*, trans. Mary Hansbury (Crestwood, NY: St. Vladimir's Seminary Press, 1989), 12.

2. See His Holiness the Dalai Lama, *Beyond Religion: Ethics for a Whole World* (New York: Mariner Books, 2012), which describes these practices outside religious institutions.

3. Examples of contemporary literature are numerous, including Cynthia Bourgeault, *Centering Prayer and Inner Awakening* (Cambridge, MA: Cowley Publications, 2004); James Finley, *Christian Meditation: Experiencing the Presence of God, a Guide to Contemplation* (San Francisco: HarperSanFrancisco, 2005); and Martin Laird, *Into the Silent Land: A Guide to the Christian Practice of Contemplation* (New York: Oxford University Press, 2006).

4. Marguerite Porete, *Mirror of Simple Souls,* trans. Ellen Babinsky (Mahwah, NJ: Paulist Press, 1993), 201.

5. Evagrius Ponticus, *Praktikos and Chapters on Prayer,* trans. John Eudes Bamberger (Kalamazoo, MI: Cistercian Publications, 1981), 14.

6. Abraham Heschel, "A Theology of Pathos," in *The Prophets,* vol. 2 (New York: Harper & Row, 1971).

7. Ruben L. F. Habito, *Living Zen, Loving God* (Boston: Wisdom Publications, 2004), 98–99.

8. Paul F. Knitter, "Making Peace and Being Peace," in *Without Buddha I Could Not Be a Christian* (New York: Oneworld Publications, 2009).

9. *The Bhagavad Gita: A New Translation,* trans. Stephen Mitchell (Easton, PA: Harmony Books, 2002), 1:47.

10. Ibid., 9:14

11. Julian of Norwich, *Showings,* trans. with introduction by Edmund Colledge and James Walsh (New York: Paulist Press, 1978), 342.

12. Malcolm Gladwell, "Small Change: Why the Revolution Will Not Be Tweeted," *New Yorker,* October 4, 2010, http://www.newyorker.com/reporting/2010/10/04/101004fa_fact_gladwell.

13. Howard Rheingold, *The Virtual Community: Homesteading on the Electronic Frontier,* rev. ed. (Boston: MIT Press, 2000), 4–5.

14. CaringBridge, www.caringbridge.org.

15. Annette Baier, "Trust and Antitrust," *Ethics* 96, no. 2 (January 1986): 235.

16. 1 Cor. 12:12. When Christians confess in the Apostles' Creed that they believe in "the holy catholic church," the meaning of the term "catholic" is "universal."

17. Luke 7:11–17; 4:38–40; John 4:13–14.

18. Margaret Wertheim, *The Pearly Gates of Cyberspace: A History of Space from Dante to the Internet* (New York: W. W. Norton & Co., 1999), 285.

19. See Mark Heim's argument in *The Depth of the Riches: A Trinitarian Theology of Religious Ends* (Grand Rapids: Eerdmans, 2000), which contends that religions can and do share similar virtues (such as compassion, healing) even as they seek different ends.

20. Deanna A. Thompson, "Embraced by the Virtual Body of Christ,"

Huffington Post blog, April 8, 2014, http://www.huffingtonpost.com /deanna-a-thompson/embraced-by-the-virtual-b_b_5111778.html.

21. For more details about Deanna Thompson's journey of talking faith through the lens of cancer, see her book *Hoping for More: Having Cancer, Talking Faith, and Accepting Grace* (Eugene, OR: Cascade Books, 2012), esp. the chapter titled "Embraced by the Virtual Body of Christ."

22. Teresa of Avila, "Christ has No Body," available at http://www .journeywithjesus.net/poemsandprayers/692-teresa_of_avila_christ _has_no_body.

23. For information about the Maker movement, see *MAKE*, a magazine published by O'Reilly Media. Numerous articles are also available, including Justin Lahart's "Tinkering Makes Comeback Amid Crisis," *The Wall Street Journal* online, November 13, 2009; available at http://online.wsj.com/news/articles/SB125798004542744219.

24. Darby Kathleen Ray, "Self, World, and the Space Between: Community Engagement as Vocational Discernment," in David S. Cunningham, *At This Time and In This Place: Vocation and Higher Education* (New York: Oxford University Press, 2016), 301–20.

25. For more on the relationship between religious difference and common goods, see Eboo Patel, *Acts of Faith: The Story of an American Muslim, in the Struggle for the Soul of a Generation* (Boston: Beacon Press, 2010).

26. Gen. 2:15.

27. Ellen F. Davis, *Scripture, Culture, and Agriculture: An Agrarian Reading of the Bible* (Cambridge: Cambridge University Press, 2009), 26.

28. St. Benedict, *The Rule of Saint Benedict*, ed. Timothy Fry, OSB (New York: Random House, 1998), 47–48.

29. Urban Roots, http://www.urbanrootsatx.org/about/. The Food Project, http://thefoodproject.org/about/ .

30. Pierre Bourdieu, *Outline of a Theory of Practice* (Cambridge: Cambridge University Press, 1977), 15, 78.

31. Paul Connerton, *How Societies Remember*, 95.

32. Ibid., 72–73.

33. Ibid. The contrast here is not between linguistic and prelinguistic but between practices where storage is the primary way that communal memory is passed on and the practices in which "passing on" occurs in face-to-face bodied encounters.

34. Connerton defines incorporative practices to also include bodily proprieties, which are quite significant in the shaping of a culture's identity. Proprieties describe what is proper for your particular body to do (how to dress, where to place your body, etc.), given your race, gender, class. For a discussion of racialized bodily proprieties see

Mary McClintock Fulkerson, *Places of Redemption: Theology for a Worldly Church* (Oxford: Oxford University Press, 2007).

35. See ibid.

36. Adisa A. Alkebulan, "The Spiritual Essence of African American Rhetoric," in *Understanding African American Rhetoric: Classical Origins to Contemporary Innovations*, ed. Ronald L. Jackson II and Elaine B. Richardson (New York: Routledge, 2003), 23–40.

37. For views that African American worship has not recognized the erotic adequately, see Anthony B. Pinn and Dwight N. Hopkins, eds., *Loving the Body: Black Religious Studies and the Erotic* (New York: Palgrave MacMillan, 2004).

38. Nancy L. Eiesland, *The Disabled God: Toward a Liberatory Theology of Disability* (Nashville: Abingdon Press, 1994), 112.

39. One expression of this is the choice to use "people first" language in special education classifications. So one speaks not about "the mentally retarded," but "a student with Down syndrome" or "a person with learning disabilities." There are more critical perspectives that challenge "normal" discourse that would even characterize people this way. Ann A. Turnbull, H. Rutherford Turnbull, Michael L. Wehmeyer, and Karrie A. Shogren, *Exceptional Lives: Special Education in Today's Schools* (Upper Saddle River, New Jersey: Merrill, 2012), 7.

40. This shift from treating such behavior as a discipline problem to reading it as communication is a profoundly important development in special education. Turnbull et al., *Exceptional Lives*, 239, 293, 416, 267. See "Treating Problem Behaviors as Communication," in Diane Baumgart, Jeanne Johnson, and Edwin Helmstetter, *Augmentative and Alternative Communication Systems for Persons with Moderate and Severe Disabilities* (Baltimore: Paul H. Brookes Publishing, 1990), 17–38.

41. Dan McAdams, *The Redemptive Self: Stories Americans Live By* (Oxford: Oxford University Press, 2005). See esp. chap. 9, "When Redemption Fails," 241–70.

42. Judith Herman, *Trauma and Recovery* (New York: Basic Books, 1992).

43. Alan F. Segal, *Life After Death: A History of the Afterlife in Western Religion* (New York: Doubleday, 2004).

44. See, for example, Alan E. Lewis, *Between Cross and Resurrection: A Theology of Holy Saturday* (Grand Rapids: Eerdmans, 2003); Shelly Rambo, *Spirit and Trauma: A Theology of Remaining* (Louisville, KY: Westminster John Knox Press, 2010); Walter Brueggemann, "Reading from the Day 'In Between,'" in *The Shadow of Glory: Reading the New Testament after the Holocaust*, ed. Tod Linafelt (New York: Routledge, 2002), 105–16; and Cornel West, "Philosophical View of

Easter," in *The Cornel West Reader* (New York: Civitas Books, 1999), 415–20.

45. Hans Urs von Balthasar, *Daz Herz der Welt* (Zurich: Arche Verlag, 1954). ET, *Heart of the World* (San Francisco: Ignatius Press, 1979).

46. Edward R. Murrow's broadcast of "This I Believe" ran from 1951 to 1955, and it inspired a contemporary forum for public dialogue: http://thisibelieve.org/.

47. Richard Wilbur, "Love Calls Us to the Things of This World," in *Richard Wilbur New and Collected Poems* (San Diego: Harvest Books), 233.

48. Sharon V. Betcher, *Spirit and the Obligation of Social Flesh: A Secular Theology for the Global City* (New York: Fordham University Press, 2013), 130.

God: In Conclusion

1. To illustrate the importance of this point, in the Gospel of Luke (Luke 24:13–35) there is a story of two men who were walking dejectedly toward their home in the town of Emmaus. Their leader, Jesus of Nazareth, had just been executed, and it seemed that everything that they believed in was a bust, a hoax. As they walked, a stranger caught up to them and asked why they were so down. They couldn't believe this guy hadn't heard about what happened—it had been all over the news. But as they walked and talked, it turned out that he knew a great deal about history, faith, and God. As he put their sadness and anger in perspective they begin to feel something coming back to life in their hearts, just a little sense that maybe everything wasn't failed after all. When they arrived home, he kept walking, but they invited the stranger to join them for supper after the long, hot walk. When they sat down and he started tearing off chunks of pita bread to pass around with the meal, they suddenly recognized him—*it was Jesus!* And as they realized this, he smiled and left.

2. Paul Tillich, *Systematic Theology*, vol. 1 (Chicago: University of Chicago Press, 1959), 241.

3. For a discussion of the relationship between words, bodies, social arrangements, and flesh, see Mayra Rivera, *Poetics of the Flesh* (Durham, NC: Duke University Press, 2015).

4. John 10:10.

Selected Bibliography: Constructive Theology

Abraham, Susan, and Elena Procario-Foley, eds. *Frontiers in Catholic Feminist Theology: Shoulder to Shoulder*. Minneapolis: Fortress Press, 2009.

Anderson, Victor. *Creative Exchange: A Constructive Theology of African American Religious Experience*. Minneapolis: Fortress Press, 2008.

Armour, Ellen T. *Signs and Wonders: Theology after Modernity*. New York: Columbia University Press, 2016.

Baker-Fletcher, Karen. *Dancing with God: The Trinity from a Womanist Perspective*. St. Louis: Chalice Press, 2006.

Carbine, Rosemary P., and Kathleen J. Dolphin, eds. *Women, Wisdom, and Witness: Engaging Contexts in Conversation*. Collegeville, MN: Michael Glazier, 2012.

Cheng, Patrick. *From Sin to Amazing Grace: Discovering the Queer Christ*. New York: Seabury Press, 2012.

Chopp, Rebecca, and Mark L. Taylor, eds. *Reconstructing Christian Theology*. Minneapolis: Fortress Press, 1994.

Cobb, John B., *Christ in a Pluralistic Age*. Eugene, OR: Wipf and Stock, 1999.

Compier, Don H. *What Is Rhetorical Theology: Textual Practice and Public Discourse*. London: Bloomsbury T. & T. Clark, 1999.

Cone, James. *God of the Oppressed*. Rev. sub. ed. Maryknoll, NY: Orbis, 1997.

Cooey, Paula. *Willing the Good: Jesus, Dissent, and Desire*. Minneapolis: Fortress, 2006.

Copeland, Shawn. *Enfleshing Freedom: Body, Race, and Being*. Minneapolis: Fortress, 2009.

Craigo-Snell, Shannon. *The Empty Church: Theater, Theology, and Bodily Hope*. Oxford: Oxford University Press, 2016.

Evans, James. *We Have Been Believers: An African American Systematic Theology*. 2nd ed. Minneapolis: Fortress Press, 2012.

Farley, Wendy. *Gathering Those Driven Away: A Theology of Incarnation*. Louisville, KY: Westminster John Knox Press, 2011.

Fulkerson, Mary McClintock. *Places of Redemption: Theology for a Worldly Church*. Oxford: Oxford University Press, 2010.

Gonzalez, Michelle A. *Afro-Cuban Theology: Religion, Race, Culture, and Identity*. Gainesville, FL: University Press of Florida, 2009.

Grau, Marion. *Rethinking Mission in the Postcolony: Salvation, Society, and Subversion*. London: Bloomsbury T. & T. Clark Publishers, 2011.

Heltzel, Peter Goodwin. *Resurrection City: A Theology of Improvisation*. Grand Rapids, MI: Wm. B. Eerdmans Publishing Co., 2012.

Hill-Fletcher, Jeannine. *Monopoly on Salvation? A Feminist Approach to Religious Pluralism*. NY: Continuum International, 2005.

Hinze, Bradford E. *Prophetic Obedience: Ecclesiology for a Dialogical Church*. Maryknoll, NY: Orbis Books, 2016.

Hodgson, Peter C. *Liberal Theology: A Radical Vision* (Minneapolis: Fortress Press, 2007).

Hodgson, Peter C., and Robert H. King eds. *Christian Theology: An Introduction to Its Traditions and Tasks*. Minneapolis: Fortress Press, 1994.

Hopkins, Dwight N., and Linda Thomas, eds. *Walk Together Children: Black and Womanist Theologies, Church, and Theological Education*. Eugene OR: Wipf and Stock, 2010.

Jensen, David. *The Lord and Giver of Life: Perspectives on Constructive Pneumatology*. Louisville, KY: Westminster John Knox Press, 2008.

Joh, Wonhee Anne. *Heart of the Cross: A Postcolonial Christology* (Louisville, KY: Westminster John Knox Press, 2006).

Jones, Serene. *Feminist Theory and Christian Theology* (Minneapolis: Fortress Press, 2000).

Jones, Serene, and Paul Lakeland, eds. *Constructive Theology: A Contemporary Approach: A Project of the Workgroup on Constructive Theology*. Minneapolis: Fortress Press, 2005.

Kamitsuka, Margaret, ed. *The Embrace of Eros: Bodies, Desires, and Sexuality in Christian Theology*. Minneapolis: Fortress Press, 2010.

Keller, Catherine. *Cloud of the Impossible: Negative Theology and Planetary Entanglement*. New York: Columbia University Press, 2014.

Keller, Catherine, and Laurel C. Schneider, eds. *Polydoxy: Theology of Multiplicity and Relation*. London: Routledge Press, 2011.

Kwok, Pui-lan. *Hope Abundant: Third World and Indigenous Women's Theology*. Maryknoll NY: Orbis Books, 2010.

Kwok, Pui-lan, and Joerg Rieger, eds. *Occupy Religion: Theology of the Multitude*. Lanham MD: Rowan and Littlefield, 2013.

Lakeland, Paul. *The Liberation of the Laity*. London: Bloomsbury Academic, 2004.

Lee, Hyo-Dong. *Spirit, Qi, and the Multitude: A Comparative Theology for the Democracy of Creation*. New York: Fordham University Press, 2013.

Lightsey, Pamela. *Our Lives Matter: A Womanist Queer Theology*. Eugene OR: Pickwick Publications, 2015.

McFague, Sallie. *Models of God: Theology for an Ecological, Nuclear Age*. Minneapolis: Fortress Press, 1987.

———. *A New Climate for Theology: God, the World, and Global Warming*. Minneapolis: Fortress Press, 2008.

Mercadante, Linda. *Belief without Borders: Inside the Minds of the Spiritual but Not Religious*. London: Oxford University Press, 2014.

Mitchem, Stephanie Y. *African American Folk Healing*. New York: New York University Press, 2007.

Pauw, Amy Plantinga, and Serene Jones, eds. *Feminist and Womanist Essays in Reformed Dogmatics*. Louisville, KY: Westminster John Knox Press, 2011.

Perkinson, James W. *White Theology: Outing Supremacy in Modernity*. Basingstoke UK: Palgrave MacMillan, 2004.

Pinn, Anthony. *The End of God-Talk: An African American Humanist Theology*. London: Oxford University Press, 2012.

Rambo, Shelly. *Spirit and Trauma: A Theology of Remaining*. Louisville, KY: Westminster John Knox Press, 2010.

Ray, Darby, ed. *Theology That Matters: Ecology, Economy, and God*. Minneapolis: Fortress Press, 2006.

Ray, Stephen G., Jr. *Do No Harm: Social Sin and Christian Responsibility*. Minneapolis: Fortress Press, 2002.

Rieger, Joerg. *God and the Excluded: Visions and Blind Spots in Contemporary Theology*. Minneapolis: Fortress Press, 2001.

Rigby, Cynthia L. *Holding Faith: A Practical Introduction to Christian Doctrine*. Nashville: Abingdon Press, 2017.

Rivera, Mayra. *The Touch of Transcendence: A Postcolonial Theology of God*. Louisville, KY: Westminster John Knox Press, 2007.

Saracino, Michele. *Christian Anthropology: An Introduction to the Human Person*. Mahwah NJ: Paulist Press, 2015.

Schneider, Laurel C. *Beyond Monotheism: A Theology of Multiplicity*. London: Routledge Press, 2007.

Schweitzer, Don. *Jesus Christ for Contemporary Life*. Eugene OR: Cascade Books, 2012.

Tanner, Kathryn. *Christ the Key*. Cambridge: Cambridge University Press, 2010.

Taylor, Mark Lewis. *The Executed God: The Way of the Cross in Lock-down America.* 2nd ed. Minneapolis: Fortress Press, 2016.

Thatamanil, John. *The Immanent Divine: God, Creation, and the Human Predicament.* Minneapolis: Fortress Press, 2006.

Thiel, John E. *Icons of Hope: The "Last Things" in Catholic Imagination.* South Bend IN: University of Notre Dame, 2013.

Thompson, Deanna. *Hoping for More: Having Cancer, Talking Faith, Accepting Grace.* Eugene, OR: Wipf and Stock, 2012.

Wallace, Mark I. *Finding God in the Singing River.* Minneapolis: Fortress Press, 2005.

Welch, Sharon. *After Empire: The Art and Ethos of Enduring Peace.* Minneapolis: Fortress Press, 2004.

Contributors

Volume Editors, Introduction and Conclusion

Stephen G. Ray Jr. is Neal F. and Ila A. Fisher Professor of Systematic Theology at Garrett-Evangelical Theological Seminary. He is the author of *Do No Harm* (Fortress Press, 2002).

Laurel C. Schneider is Professor of Religious Studies and Women's and Gender Studies at Vanderbilt University. She is the author of *Beyond Monotheism: A Theology of Multiplicity* (Routledge, 2007) and *Re-Imagining the Divine: Confronting the Backlash against Feminist Theology* (Pilgrim Press, 1998).

What Do We Know and How? Context and Questions

Shannon Craigo-Snell is Professor of Theology, Louisville Presbyterian Theological Seminary. She is author of *The Empty Church: Theater, Theology, and Bodily Hope* (Oxford University Press, 2014); *Silence, Love, and Death: Saying "Yes" to God in the Theology of Karl Rahner* (Marquette University Press, 2008) and coauthor (with Shawnthea Monroe) of *Living Christianity: A Pastoral Theology for Today* (Fortress Press, 2009).

Joerg Rieger is Cal Turner Chancellor's Chair in Wesleyan Studies and Distinguished Professor of Theology at Vanderbilt

University Divinity School. His most recent books include *Unified We Are a Force: How Faith and Labor Can Overcome America's Inequalities* (with Rosemarie Henkel-Rieger; Chalice Press, 2016); *Faith on the Road: A Short Theology of Travel and Justice* (IVP Academic, 2015); *Occupy Religion: Theology of the Multitude* (with Kwok Pui-lan; Rowman & Littlefield Publishers, 2012); *Globalization and Theology* (Abingdon Press, 2010); and *No Rising Tide: Theology, Economics, and the Future* (Fortress Press, 2009).

Cynthia L. Rigby is the W. C. Brown Professor of Theology at Austin Presbyterian Theological Seminary. She is the author of *Holding Faith: A Practical Introduction to Christian Doctrine* (Abingdon Press, 2016).

Kathleen Sands is Associate Professor of American Studies, University of Hawai'i at Mānoa. She is author of *Escape from Paradise: Evil and Tragedy in Feminist Theology* (Fortress Press, 1990) and editor of *God Forbid: Religion and Sex in American Public Life* (Oxford University Press, 2000).

Tradition in Action

Jeannine Hill Fletcher is Professor of Theology, Fordham University. She is author of *Monopoly on Salvation? A Feminist Approach to Religious Pluralism* (Bloomsbury Academic, 2005) and *Motherhood as Metaphor: Engendering Interreligious Dialogue* (Fordham University Press, 2013).

Peter Goodwin Heltzel is Associate Professor of Systematic Theology and Director of the Micah Institute at New York Theological Seminary. He is the author of *Resurrection City: A Theology of Improvisation* (Eerdmans, 2012) and *Jesus and Justice: Evangelicals, Race, and American Politics* (Yale University Press, 2009).

Kris Kvam is Associate Professor of Theology, Saint Paul School of Theology.

Hyo-Dong Lee is Associate Professor of Comparative Theology, Drew University Theological School. He is author of *Spirit,*

Qi, and the Multitude: A Comparative Theology for the Democracy of Creation (Fordham University Press, 2013).

John Thatamanil is Associate Professor of Theology and World Religions at Union Theological Seminary in the City of New York. He is the author of *The Immanent Divine: God, Creation, and the Human Predicament* (Fortress Press, 2006).

Ways of World-Making

Rosemary P. Carbine is Associate Professor of Religious Studies at Whittier College. Along with contributing numerous articles in major scholarly journals and anthologies, she has coedited and contributed chapters to *The Gift of Theology: The Contribution of Kathryn Tanner* (Fortress Press, 2015); *Theological Perspectives for Life, Liberty, and the Pursuit of Happiness: Public Intellectuals for the Twenty-First Century* (Palgrave Macmillan, 2013); and *Women, Wisdom, and Witness: Engaging Contexts in Conversation* (Liturgical Press, 2012).

Don Compier is Dean of the Bishop Kemper School for Ministry in Topeka, Kansas. He also serves as Canon Theologian of the Episcopal Diocese of Kansas. He is associate priest for Latino ministry at St. Paul's Episcopal Church, Kansas City, Kansas. Dr. Compier has published several books, including *Listening to Popular Music* (Fortress Press, 2013), selected as one of the ten best books in ethics in the annual book review issue of *The Christian Century*, and a coedited volume, *Empire and the Christian Tradition* (Fortress Press, 2007), which was named the best reference book of the year by the Academy of Parish Clergy.

Wendy Farley is Professor of Christian Spirituality and Director of the Program in Christian Spirituality, San Francisco Theological Seminary. She is the author of *The Thirst of God: Contemplating God's Love with Three Women Mystics* (Westminster John Knox Press, 2015) and *Gathering Those Driven Away: A Theology of Incarnation* (Westminster John Knox Press, 2011).

Marion Grau is Professor of Systematic Theology and Missiology and the Director of the Egede Institute at the MF

Norwegian School of Theology in Oslo, Norway. She is the author of *Refiguring Theological Hermeneutics: Hermes, Trickster, Fool* (Palgrave MacMillan, 2014); *Rethinking Mission in the Postcolony: Salvation, Society and Subversion* (T. & T. Clark, 2011); *Of Divine Economy: Refinancing Redemption* (T. & T. Clark, 2004); and editor (with Rosemary Radford Ruether) of *Interpreting the Postmodern: Responses to Radical Orthodoxy* (T. & T. Clark, 2006).

David H. Jensen is Academic Dean and Professor in the Clarence N. and Betty B. Frierson Distinguished Chair of Reformed Theology, Austin Presbyterian Theological Seminary. His research and teaching interests explore the interconnections between Christian theology and daily life. His most recent books include *God, Desire, and a Theology of Human Sexuality* and *1 and 2 Samuel*, both published by Westminster John Knox Press.

Mary McClintock Fulkerson is Professor of Theology, Duke Divinity School. She is the author of *Places of Redemption: Theology for a Worldly Church* (Oxford University Press, 2010) and coeditor (with Sheila Briggs) of *The Oxford Handbook of Feminist Theology* (Oxford University Press, 2014).

Linda Mercadante is the B. Robert Straker Chair of Historical Theology at Methodist Theological School in Ohio. She is an ordained minister in the Presbyterian Church (U.S.A.), a Fellow of The Center of Theological Inquiry and The Collegeville Institute, and the founding member of the unit on Religious Conversions of the American Academy of Religion. She has written five books and over fifty articles, the most recent being *Belief without Borders: Inside the Minds of the Spiritual but Not Religious* (Oxford University Press, 2014).

James W. Perkinson is Professor of Social Ethics and Theology, Ecumenical Theological Seminary. He is the author of *White Theology: Outing Supremacy in Modernity* (Palgrave

Macmillan, 2004) and *Messianism against Christology: Resistance Movements, Folk Arts, and Empire* (Palgrave Macmillan, 2013).

Shelley Rambo is Associate Professor of Theology, Boston University School of Theology. She is the author of *Spirit and Trauma: A Theology of Remaining* (Westminster John Knox Press, 2010).

Darby Kathleen Ray is Donald W. and Ann M. Harward Professor of Civic Engagement, Bates College. She is the author of *Working* (Fortress Press, 2011); *Incarnation and Imagination: A Christian Ethic of Ingenuity* (Fortress, 2008); and *Deceiving the Devil: Atonement, Abuse, and Ransom* (Pilgrim Press, 1998).

Mayra Rivera is Professor of Theology and Latino/a Studies, Harvard University. She is the author of *Poetics of the Flesh* (Duke University Press, 2015), and *The Touch of Transcendence: A Postcolonial Theology of God* (Westminster John Knox Press, 2007).

Don Schweitzer is the McDougald Professor of Theology at St. Andrew's College, Saskatoon, Canada. He is an ordained minister in The United Church of Canada and has published in the areas of Christology and the Holy Spirit.

Deanna Thompson is Professor of Religion, Hamline University. She is the author of *Hoping for More: Having Cancer, Talking Faith, and Accepting Grace* (Wipf and Stock, 2012) and *Deuteronomy* (Westminster John Knox Press, 2014).

Mark I. Wallace is Professor of Religion and Environmental Studies at Swarthmore College, Pennsylvania. He is the author of *Green Christianity: Five Ways to a Sustainable Future* (Fortress, 2010); *Finding God in the Singing River: Christianity, Spirit, Nature* (Fortress, 2005); *Fragments of the Spirit: Nature, Violence, and the Renewal of Creation* (Continuum, 1996; Trinity, 2002); and *The Second Naiveté: Barth, Ricoeur, and the New Yale Theology* (Mercer University Press, 1995). He is editor of Paul Ricoeur's *Figuring the Sacred: Religion, Narrative, and Imagination* (Fortress,

1995) and coeditor of *Curing Violence: Essays on René Girard* (Polebridge, 1994).

Additional Contributions

Sheila Briggs is Associate Professor of Religion and Associate in the Gender Studies Program, University of Southern California. She is coeditor (with Mary McClintock Fulkerson) of *The Oxford Handbook of Feminist Theology* (Oxford University Press, 2014).

James H. Evans is Robert K. Davies Professor of Systematic Theology at Colgate Rochester Crozier Divinity School. He is the author of *We Shall All Be Changed* (1997); *Modern Christian Thought: The Twentieth Century*, 2nd edition (2006); and *Playing: Christian Explorations of Daily Living* (2010), all published by Fortress Press.

Sharon Welch is Provost and Professor of Religion and Society at Meadville Lombard Theological School. She is the author of *Real Peace, Real Security: The Challenges of Global Citizenship* (Fortress Press, 2008) and *After Empire: The Art and Ethos of Enduring Peace* (Fortress Press, 2004).

Index

CPSIA information can be obtained
at www.ICGtesting.com
Printed in the USA
FSHW010041080919
61792FS